Also by Linda Albert

Coping with Kids

Coping with Kids and School

Coping with Kids and Vacation
(with Elaine Shimberg)

Strengthening Your Stepfamily
(with Elizabeth Einstein)

Also by Michael Popkin

*Active Parenting: Teaching Cooperation,
Courage and Responsibility*

"So . . . Why Aren't You Perfect Yet?"

QUALITY PARENTING

QUALITY PARENTING

How to Transform
the Everyday Moments
We Spend with Our Children
into Special,
Meaningful Time

Linda Albert & Michael Popkin

Random House 🏠 *New York*

All rights reserved under International and Pan-American Copyright
Conventions. Published in the United States by Random House, Inc.,
New York, and simultaneously in Canada by Random House of Canada
Limited, Toronto.

Library of Congress Cataloging-in-Publication Data

Albert, Linda.
Quality parenting.

1. Parent and child. 2. Parenting.
I. Popkin, Michael, 1950–   . II. Title.
HQ755.85.A38   1987   649.1   87-12703
ISBN 0-394-55744-1

Manufactured in the United States of America
24689753
First Edition

To Judith, Steven, and Ken,
for all the past and future memorable moments
that make being your mother such a splendid experience

Linda Albert

To Melody, my quality parenting partner,
and to our daughter, Megan,
who makes it so worthwhile

Michael Popkin

ACKNOWLEDGMENTS

Books, like families, need support systems in order to survive. We'd like to thank the many people who provided that support during the process of writing this book.

Without the unending assistance of Charlotte Mayerson, our editor at Random House, the writing would have been over before it began. Charlotte nursed the book (and us) through the initial proposal and development stage, watched over us during the research and writing, and then prodded us as needed to make the manuscript the very best it could be. It wasn't always easy for any of us, and we thank her for never giving up.

For their encouragement and understanding during the many long days and weekends spent working, we thank Byron Eakin and Melody Popkin.

To our colleagues and peer consultants in the professional world, especially those involved in the North American Society for Adlerian Psychology, our thanks for the knowledge and inspiration that helped us formulate the ideas presented in this book.

Special thanks go to the many individuals and families who so willingly shared their lives and memories with us.

We appreciate the efforts of our research assistants, Elizabeth Gilliom and Chris LaBudde, for their diligent work on this project, and to Judith Rachel for her valuable suggestions. Thanks to Pam Bernstein of the William Morris Agency for all her efforts on our behalf. Finally to our parents, from whom we received our first training for quality parenting, thank you.

PREFACE

The original idea for *Quality Parenting* surfaced during a conversation that Linda had with Elizabeth Crow, editor in chief of *Parents Magazine*.

"I'm looking for an article," explained Elizabeth, "that tells working parents, mothers especially, that it's okay to have a career and a family. But I also want to tell them that even though they might spend eight hours a day at the office, they can also maintain close, caring family ties."

For years Linda, a professional writer and teacher, had been doing just that—pursuing her busy career while bringing up three active children. What was it that made this balance possible? What was it that fostered that special family warmth even in the tightest time crunch? Linda thought back to a favorite phrase of psychologists: "It's not the quantity of time you spend with your kids that counts, it's the quality that matters." What made the difference for Linda was quality time—the time she spent with her kids in a special closeness that is still remembered years later.

What followed was a series of how-to articles on the subject of quality time in *Parents Magazine.* Clarifying the concept of quality time and breaking it down into its component parts so that other parents could make use of it proved to be a difficult task, however. Virtually no other information on the subject was available. When Linda decided to expand the idea into book-length format, she interviewed many family-life "experts"—social workers, parenting educators, and psychologists—who frequently made use of the term "quality time" to describe optimal family interactions.

None could define quality time in specific terms: What is it? How do you get it? How do you know when you've had it?

One of the parenting educators that Linda queried was Michael Popkin, author and publisher of *Active Parenting: A Video-Based Program.* Michael suggested that the way to find more information about quality time would be to ask the real experts on the subject—the mothers, fathers, and kids who have experienced quality time in their own families. A rewarding partnership developed.

We interviewed over three hundred families, asking parents to think about special experiences from their own childhood. We asked teens and children to talk about recent memorable experiences in their lives. We asked everybody interviewed to identify the factors that made these memories special for them. We then analyzed the memories, looking for the specifics that would enable us to understand the quality time concept in all its dimensions.

The results delighted us. Not only did we learn a variety of specific memorable activities, many of which are included in this book, but we also uncovered many of the underlying skills, attitudes, and special elements (which we call "QP" factors) that make quality experiences possible. It was at this time that we realized that we were really talking about *quality parenting,* a much broader concept than quality time.

The information we gathered allowed us to go beyond the typical "recipe" books of activities for parents and children. Recipe books are certainly useful—we wouldn't step into the kitchen without one. That's why we've included two chapters of specific activities in this book. But just as some cooks can turn a recipe into a delicious meal, other cooks can turn the same recipe into a disaster.

The difference between success and disaster, as we have discovered through our research, consists of particular skills, attitudes, and "QP" factors. These will not only help you make any recipe successful but will also enable you to create new quality experiences for your family.

We've woven direct quotes and stories from the research participants into the text of the book. While we've changed names to preserve anonymity, in most instances we've kept the wording exactly as it was given to us. We thought readers would enjoy the feel of hearing real people talk.

The research style we employed is journalistic rather than scientific. By investigating what is already happening in families and looking for the common principles that make quality parenting possible, we have aimed for a book that is both immediate and practical.

We believe that parenting is one of the most important jobs a person can do. Parenting also has the potential to be one of the most rewarding life experiences. Yet for too many families this potential isn't fully realized. What goes wrong between the enthusiasm of the baby shower and the relief of the high school graduation?

Often the difficulty stems from a lack of an appropriate balance between the need for disciplinary guidance and the enjoyment of the rich, loving relationship between us and our children.

The discipline task often seems so overwhelming that many parents find very little time, energy, or interest left for the more rewarding side of parenting that we call quality parenting. Look at the shelves of any neighborhood bookstore. You'll find loads of books devoted to discipline (we've written several of these books ourselves) but few, if any, on quality parenting. It's obvious that this side of the parenting ledger has been neglected. How ironic, for when families enjoy more quality experiences, the kids need less discipline.

This book, then, is not only for your children but also to enrich your own life. Our wish is that you and your family grow in closeness and caring as you implement the ideas on the pages that follow.

Linda Albert   Michael Popkin

CONTENTS

Chapter 5　Playing ╎ *62*

Why Many Parents Don't Play • Participating • Making
the Time • Being There • Letting It Out • Tuning in to
Your Child's Delight

Chapter 6　Teaching ╎ *70*

Motivation • Timing • Demonstration • Practicing • Acknowledging Efforts • Teaching the Teacher • Teaching
Values

Chapter 7　Making Time for Quality Parenting ╎ *80*

Time-Management Principle 1: Make and Use "To Do"
Lists • Time-Management Principle 2: Alter the Frequency
of Performing Routine Tasks • Time-Management
Principle 3: Beware of Diminishing Returns •
Time-Management Principle 4: Be Willing to
Timeshift • Time-Management Principle 5: K.I.S.S. (Keep
It Short and Simple) • Time-Management Principle 6:
Chunk It, Don't Chuck It • Time-Management Principle 7:
Make a Written Schedule • Time-Management Principle
8: Delegate Responsibility • Cooperation: The Key to
Family Efficiency • The List • Distributing Chores • Tips
for Handling Chores

Chapter 8　Quality Time at Any Time ╎ *97*

Quality Parenting in the Morning • Quality Parenting
Before Dinner • Quality Parenting at the Dinner
Table • Quality Parenting at Bedtime • Quality Parenting
During Travel Time

Chapter 9　Quality Parenting at Special Times ╎ *117*

Special Considerations • Prime-Time TV • Game Time •
Family Council Meetings • Dining Out • Dining In •
Holidays and Family Gatherings • Family Outings
• Vacations • Making Memories

QUALITY PARENTING

Chapter 1

THE CONCEPT OF QUALITY PARENTING

Who hasn't heard the platitude "It's not the quantity of time you spend with your kids that counts, it's the quality?" Yet as familiar as this concept is, we realized, no one had ever really defined "quality time" or shown parents how this worthwhile goal could be achieved. So we set out to conduct an in-depth exploration of this popular notion.

Our first step was to interview over three hundred parents around the country. We found that even though all of them were familiar with the concept of quality time, few of the parents could say exactly what they thought it was.

"Quality time," explained one mother from Laredo, Texas, "happens in those moments when my son and I are on the same wavelength, when neither of us is distracted or thinking about anything else."

A dad from Atlanta was a little more poetic in defining it. "It's those unexpected bursts of genuine rapport."

One parent answered: "I feel like I'm the best parent when I spend time with my kids and I am not being judgmental or evaluative or reprimanding them. There are no right or wrong answers during that time."

One of our favorite definitions is an analogy made by a

California parent: "Quality time is like feeding my kids a healthy diet high in natural foods and vitamins. It sustains the kids throughout the day when I have to be busy elsewhere. Without quality time it's like feeding my kids a junk-food diet. They eat a lot but they're never satisfied."

In analyzing these and other responses, we realized that the original concept for this book needed to be expanded. Although the idea of quality time is useful, a concept was needed that went beyond the idea of time—a concept that also encompassed the skills, attitudes, and behaviors that combine to make parenting a positive experience. We realized that what we were really investigating was quality parenting itself.

Why Quality Parenting?

Planning and achieving quality parenting grows increasingly difficult. Almost all fathers and well over half of all mothers work outside the home. If you are one of these working parents, you know the guilt you feel when you are not at home with your kids. When Alicia wins her tennis match or Kevin takes his first step, you feel strong pangs of regret that your work kept you from being there. You don't have time to waste—every minute counts. Most parents are anxious to turn many of the ordinary, everyday moments they spend with their kids into high-quality interactions. Divorced parents or stepparents who don't live with their kids seven days a week especially want to know how to make the most of their time together.

Even if you're home with your kids all day every day, you will benefit from knowing what quality parenting is and how to achieve more of it. Without this information it's too easy to fall into the trap of just "being there," substituting long periods of uninvolved coexistence for really being together.

"I talk but my parents never hear me," declared one twelve-year-old junior-high student. "They're too busy to help me." This young man was expressing a need to be heard, accepted, and loved. Emphasizing quality parenting will help him feel that his parents care, that he is an important part of their lives.

Families that do emphasize quality parenting often develop a marvelous sense of closeness and respect for each other. Interpersonal problems don't get out of hand. It's hard to carry a grudge against someone when you're laughing together, and the spontaneous talk that occurs during such times often leads to spontaneous solutions.

Myths and Misconceptions

Quality parenting is not simply playing games. You don't have to love Monopoly or Scrabble or Trivial Pursuit to be an effective parent. Nor does sharing good times together mean you have to do artsy-craftsy projects with your kids. One parent complained, "I hate the whole notion of quality parenting. When I come home from work I don't want to take out the craft supplies and have the kids make a mess all over the kitchen. I don't want to have to help them be creative. I just want to get dinner on the table."

You do not have to provide constant entertainment for your kids. Many parents, especially divorced ones, fall prey to the Saturday Parent Syndrome. These parents spend their time with their children doing as many "fun" things as possible. They go from the zoo to McDonald's to a movie all in a few short hours. In this frantic rush to "fit it all in" they are likely to sacrifice quality, not achieve it.

Neither is it necessary that rewarding encounters with your children always be spontaneous. While it's true that some of the most delightful moments families share occur when least expected, most of them happen when parents set the stage. Subsequent chapters of this book show you how to do exactly that.

It's a mistake to think of quality parenting as part of today's trend toward "quick fixes." The goal is not to spend as little time as possible with your kids, nor to get your time together over with so you can pretend they aren't around. Rather it's a way to make the most of the time you do share.

Finally, it's not important that everyone in the family take part in every activity. You'll want to balance time spent one-on-one with time spent all together.

The Truth About Quality Parenting

Quality parenting, as defined in this book, is a way of life. It's the means by which we can transform the ordinary, every-day moments we spend with our kids into special, meaningful times that foster feelings of closeness, caring, and understanding.

Positive interaction is the key. Thirty minutes spent silently watching TV together has less quality than two minutes expressing thoughts and feelings during a commercial break. Relationships often seem empty and nonfulfilling because the emphasis is on social contact, not psychological contact. It's not the Scrabble game played by father and daughter that is valuable, it's the talk about the day's events, the jokes they share, or perhaps just the smiles they exchange.

Quality parenting is not something you do *to* or *for* your child but rather something you do *with* your child. The ideas in the chapters that follow will show you ways to make psychological contact with your youngsters throughout the day.

How do you know when quality parenting is occurring?

The feeling is as elusive—and as elating—as being in love. "I know by the glow" is how one parent explains it. Another says, "There's a spark of excitement, a zing of energy in the air." Most parents we interviewed could identify the occasions when they felt relaxed, fulfilled, loving, close to their children, and happy. Many also noted a marked absence of anger, resentment, and guilt.

How you feel about yourself is a clue to recognizing quality parenting. Typically, parents feel good about themselves and their ability to parent during these times. They also feel good about their relationship with their children. "It was during one such experience," said a dad from New York, "that I realized how much I like my kid."

Sometimes your kids will identify an experience of quality by their reaction. Their words and body language tell you that they feel close to you. When it's over, they may express their appreciation by giving you a spontaneous hug. If they ask to repeat the activity or experience again soon, you know it was a winner.

As we've already seen, one mother described quality parenting as healthy food that sustains a child throughout the day. Many parents elaborated on the idea of sustenance by reporting that they know they are achieving appropriate amounts of quality parenting when their kids no longer clamor for attention by constant misbehavior or interruptions. Their children get their fill of family love and, satisfied, go to sleep at night with ease.

We've found this exercise most illuminating in our own families and also in the families of the people we've worked with. Sit around the dinner table some night and play "Do You Remember?" The game is simple. Everyone responds by describing family events or shared times they remember with pleasure and wish could happen again soon. Do this often and you'll know exactly what qualifies as quality parenting in your house.

The 10 Percent Principle

High-quality interactions are often thought of as peak experiences that stand out from the ordinary routine of daily living. When parents talk about the glow that comes over them and their children during such experiences they are bearing witness to this wonderful phenomenon.

Quality parenting is not, however, an either-or phenomenon: either you are "doing it" or you are not. It is rather a part of a continuum that runs from low-quality interactions to those of very high quality. We all have good times and bad with our children. What we're aiming for in this book is to help us all achieve the understanding, skills, and attitudes that will give us more of the higher-quality experience.

People are not going to spend 100 percent of their time with their children in quality parenting. It's simply not possible. It's more realistic to aim to increase experiences of quality parenting by 10 percent with each child and to improve the quality of all family interactions—quality or not—by 10 percent.

Ten percent may not seem like a lot of change, but the payoffs for you and your child can be enormous. Think of the time spent with your child as an investment in a sort of sacred savings account. The more quality you put in, the healthier your child will grow, and the more you have to draw against during those times of conflict when your role as a parent requires you to discipline your child.

Of course, you will have to have something in the account if you are going to make withdrawals. The beauty of the 10 percent principle is like the magic of compound interest. By continuing to add 10 percent to the quality of your time together, you will very rapidly build up that very special account over time. Five years down the road the difference will be phenomenal.

Test Yourself

How can we evaluate which activities or interactions help us in quality parenting and which do not? Let's look at the following vignettes. Similar situations have probably occurred in your family, just as they have in ours. As you read, try to rate each one on a scale of 1 to 100, from negative parenting at 1 to 39, to ordinary parenting at 40 to 69, to superb parenting at 70 to 100.

1. Julia and Marco are skipping along the woodsy path about fifty feet in front of you. You've been in the park for over an hour. Generally the kids have been by themselves up ahead or around the next curve. You and your spouse are walking much more slowly, enjoying the chance to chat with each other for a change. Each time one of the kids comes back to ask you a question or to show you a leaf or a rock you respond, "That's nice, dear. Now go and play while we talk."

2. It's time to tuck Nicole into bed. Tonight you spend an extra five minutes with her, asking how she handled the situation with her friend Lisa, who has been snubbing her lately in the hall between classes. She tells you how angry and upset she feels when this happens. You listen with sympathy, accepting her feelings without judgment or criticism. Then you share with her a similar experience from your own childhood.

3. It's four o'clock Saturday afternoon. The whole family is gathered to spend an hour together. The twins, Tommy and Marie, are watching *Sesame Street.* You are correcting math papers from your fifth-grade students and your spouse is reading the paper.

4. As you enter the kitchen for your morning cup of coffee, fifteen-year-old Daniel is wolfing down the last bite of

toast and peanut butter before he darts out the door to catch the school bus. You put your arm around his shoulder and say, "Glad to see you this morning. Thanks for helping out in the yard last night. It's wonderful to have a son as capable as you are."

5. Supper will be ready in five minutes. Meanwhile, everyone is seated around the table holding your best crystal wineglasses filled with grape juice. "To Ricky," you begin the toast, "for his successful achievement of a B-plus on his science project." Everybody clinks glasses, looks at Ricky, and drinks the juice. The toast is repeated so Jenny can snap a picture of this special moment.

How Did You Score?

We'd rate vignette 1, the walk in the woods, in the mid-range, about 40 to 60. All the potential for high-quality parenting is there—the family is all together, taking part in a special activity that everyone enjoys. What this experience lacks, however, is positive parent-child interaction that involves the sharing of thoughts, ideas, experiences, and feelings. As so often happens on family outings, the kids are doing their own thing while their parents' attention is focused elsewhere. The quality of this activity would increase if everyone walked together at the same pace or in adult-child pairs. Holding hands and exploring the wonders of the woods together would also increase the closeness. A playful chase, a game of hide-and-seek, or a roll down a hillside that would leave everyone breathless and laughing could add even more quality to this scene.

Vignette 2, putting Nicole to bed, falls into the quality parenting range—around 75 to 80. Even though the entire activity takes only five minutes, feelings and experiences are expressed by both parent and child. One way to increase the quality of this situation would be to increase the clock time by five or ten minutes and continue the already excellent interaction.

We'd rate vignette 3, Saturday afternoon with the twins, as ordinary time, somewhere in the 30 to 70 range. If there's little interaction while the TV is on, the rating is close to 30. The more interaction that occurs, the higher the rating. Even though this family is gathered together, they share little. Each person in the family is in his or her own little world. If, when *Sesame Street* ends, the parents stop what they are doing and focus on their kids for a moment, they can use the program as a stimulus for interacting. They can talk about what was shown on TV, perhaps sing some *Sesame Street* songs together, or even read from the *Sesame Street* magazine. For some fun they can take turns imitating Big Bird or Cookie Monster or Oscar the Grouch.

Vignette 4, "the hasty breakfast," falls into the higher-quality range, between 70 and 80, even though the clock time involved is probably less than two minutes. During this simple transaction, the arm around the shoulder is a demonstration of affection; "Glad to see you this morning" is an expression of feeling; "Thanks for helping out in the yard last night" is a statement of appreciation; and "It's wonderful to have a son as capable as you are" affirms the child's importance in the family as well as highlighting his successes. Such short interactions of good quality are a godsend to busy parents.

Vignette 5 also rates in the quality parenting range, probably around 80 or 90. Kids love celebrations of all sorts. There's fun in drinking out of the best crystal glasses, in pretending grape juice is wine, in acting grown-up and important. Celebrations also give families a unique history that will be fondly remembered by everyone long after the kids have grown. The pictures Jenny snapped of the event will give the family pleasure whenever the family picture album is opened. Finally, acknowledging Ricky's good grades and making him the focus of family admiration is bound to boost his self-esteem.

Making It Happen

Our research suggests a number of ways to analyze quality parenting in order to make it happen. First, several factors seemed to be very important to the kids. We call these the QP factors: parents spend time alone with each child; the child is the center of attention; the whole family does it together; kids can count on it; parents put kids' needs first; parents show they care; kids feel grown-up; everyone is relaxed; and parents make it fun. In Chapter 2, we'll look at how these QP factors and the accompanying attitudes can help you apply the 10 percent principle we talked about earlier.

Another way to make quality parenting happen more often is to polish and refine your skills of sharing, encouraging, playing, and teaching. These skills are specific tools for making experiences with your child more memorable. Chapters 3, 4, 5, and 6 give you the information you need to be able to develop and use these skills effectively.

We know, from talking to hundreds of parents about quality experiences, that the biggest obstacle is the time crunch. The daily schedule, especially for parents who work outside of the home, makes very heavy demands. To ease this burden, we've included in Chapter 7 time-management strategies that can save precious minutes when parents are at home with their children.

This will give you more time to enjoy some of the specific activities suggested in Chapters 8 and 9. We've combined the QP factors, attitudes, and skills into specific how-to's for various times of the day, week, and year: morning, mealtime, before and after dinner, bedtime, travel time, weekends, vacations, and holidays. You'll find over fifty activities to choose from. They may also stimulate you to design other activities that will be unique to your family.

If you are a single parent or live in any type of blended family, Chapter 10 contains specific applications of the quality parenting concept for you. The sections on tips for single parents and tips for stepparents will help you initiate quality parenting in your families.

In Chapter 11, we answer questions that parents asked us when we were doing the research for this book.

The Quality Parenting Action Plan, the final chapter, puts it all together. Here you can take pen and paper in hand and come up with a blueprint that will help you bridge the gap between good intentions and successful action.

Quality Parenting is written like a guidebook. Start anywhere you like and proceed in any direction. You can repeat ideas and activities as often as you wish. Ignore the suggestions that don't appeal to you and modify others to suit your individual taste.

Quality in any form adds richness to our lives. It is our hope that the ideas presented in this book will enable you to achieve more fully the satisfaction that comes from quality parenting.

Chapter 2

THE QP FACTORS

What separates quality parenting from other types of contact that we have with our children? When we began the research for this book, we discovered that from the kids' point of view, such times were not necessarily related to any specific activity. We asked the youngsters we interviewed to describe one quality experience in their families. Then we asked, "What made this particular event special to you?" In analyzing their answers, we discovered that a number of factors occurred over and over again. These QP factors, as we call them, seem to form an underlying framework for quality parenting.

From our experience with our own children, we suspect that the parents of the children and teens we interviewed were not aware of these factors at the time they were happening. But by becoming aware of these QP factors, we can better plan future activities. Incorporating even one of them into an activity is very likely to increase its quality.

Parents Spend Time Alone with Each Child

> Before school started last year, Mom took one afternoon just for
> me. We shopped for clothes and got some school supplies and
> then we had lunch together and talked about everything. I was
> the only thing on her mind. She's usually so busy with day-to-
> day stuff and with taking care of my father and my brothers
> that it's hard for us to have any time alone together. She had
> a big smile on her face when I thanked her for the good time
> I had. I think that day had a lot to do with our getting along
> much better than we used to.

Some of the best moments for children happen when they
do something alone with a parent. Perhaps it's because this
one-to-one time satisfies a child's need to feel uniquely loved
and significant. We know as adults that when someone
spends time with us, it's a compliment. It says, "I value you.
You're worth taking time for." For children "invited" by
their parents, such feelings are probably many times
stronger. After all, to a child a parent is the most important
person in the world.

One of the hardest things any child ever has to do is share
his or her parents. Rose, the oldest of seven, and now an
adult, put it this way:

> There was always a baby in the house demanding Mom's atten-
> tion. She'd try to talk to me but one of the other kids always
> interrupted. The only time I remember being alone with her
> was when we went shopping together, and even then she was
> busy picking stuff out.

For children with siblings, this need for one-to-one time
with a parent, away from brothers and sisters, is especially
strong. One-on-one time offers a welcome respite from competition for a parent's attention and makes it easier for children to cooperate with each other. It's not surprising,

therefore, that many psychologists recommend spending such time with each child as a way to decrease sibling rivalry.

Even only children don't have their parents' undivided attention very often. There are a thousand and one things that demand our time and energy throughout the day, and unless there's a problem, we may not take the time to focus on the child. Even a few minutes of attention can make an impact, as Toni says:

> Every morning my mom makes breakfast just for me. I think that's great because I have time to sit down and eat with her and talk about what's on my mind.

What did the children we interviewed like doing alone with their parents? Their responses ran the gamut—playing games, going to sporting events, eating out, walking in the woods, watching TV, sharing a hobby, fishing. Yet, over and over, the children repeated that it wasn't the activity itself that was the key factor, but rather the talking that accompanied it. Lisa, who used to caddy for her dad, wasn't really interested in golf.

> On the weekends Dad would take me with him when he played golf alone. I always thought that it was really neat to be on the golf course. He let me drive the golf cart even though I wasn't very old. It was fun because there was just the two of us, and we could talk all we wanted.

The implications of this QP factor—they spend time alone with me—seems clear. We can chose any activity we and our child want to do. What's crucial is that we both choose to be there and that no distractions interfere. And, while together, we keep on talking and sharing.

The Child Is the Center of Attention

> My mom is a teacher and we have "show and tell" at home just
> like kids do at school. We take turns, each one doing "show and
> tell" on a different night. Wednesday is my night. I save up my
> good papers from the week and pass them around. I read out
> loud from my reader. Then I tell them the best things that
> happened to me during the week. I love this time best because
> everybody—even my brothers and sisters—is listening and
> being nice to me.

Children bask in the warmth of their family's undivided
attention like sunbathers in the sun. Such focused appreciation helps to strengthen a child's sense of importance and
serves as a reminder that she or he is a valued member of the
family. But just as persistent sunbathing can be harmful, so
can constant attention. It's the occasional stardom that enhances a child's self-esteem and serves as a quality experience. Judy had just such an experience during her junior
year in high school:

> I had a small but important part in the school play. My mother
> was big on photographs so she came to the dress rehearsal and
> shot two whole roles of pictures—seventy-two of them. One of
> my friends asked if he could have some copies once they were
> developed. "Sure," my mom said, "but you need to know that
> every one of these pictures is of Judy." My friend's mouth
> dropped open. "You shot seventy-two pictures just of Judy?"
> That's my mom! She loved my plays and made sure that every-
> one in the family saw all those stacks of pictures of me. It made
> me feel like I was a star! Like I really had talent.

Birthdays, graduations, confirmations, and performances
naturally lead to making children the center of everyone's
attention. However, we can also give special attention to our
children for the more ordinary successes of their everyday
lives: a good grade on a paper, a book read, a well-played

basketball game, a chore remembered. Such attention also helps strengthen kids' motivation to continue their efforts. After all, the roar of the crowd—or the flash of seventy-two of Mother's bulbs—has kept many an actress learning her lines until the next curtain came up.

The Whole Family Does It Together

> Every summer we freeze tons of strawberries. We get up while it's still dark and then drive to the farm and pick and pick and pick. Mom has to pay extra for all the berries we eat. Then we go home and set up the assembly line—somebody washes, somebody slices, somebody bags, somebody puts syrup in. We try to see how fast we can go and end up racing all around the kitchen. The neat thing is that we do it all together—we have separate jobs but we are really part of the same thing.

Doing things together as a family is important to children. The psychiatrist Alfred Adler made the observation that people come into this world with few skills and a profound sense of helplessness. It's not surprising, then, that Adler concluded that the most fundamental human need is to belong. During our early years it is only by belonging that we can survive. As we grow, the feeling that we belong and are part of a group is essential to our emotional health.

A strong sense of belonging is therefore important for a child's development. Doing things as a family contributes to it and provides kids with a warmth and security that can last a lifetime. Family traditions, religious services, shared vacations, Sunday nights at a favorite neighborhood restaurant— all define for the child the uniqueness of his or her particular family. They provide the child with a sense of identity and a feeling that he or she is part of a well-defined group— because this is what we do together. As Tony says:

We go to the mountains every summer. Sometimes we stop by a stream and play on the rocks. When we get hungry we have a picnic and then go wading in the water. At the hotel, we order room service and eat in the room. It's always real special for us. My mom and dad and I are all in one room together, playing cards or something. I like that because we are together without anybody else around or doing separate stuff.

This sense that their family is a unique group gives children an identity bigger than themselves. Such an identity can help children learn that one person's problem is everybody's problem, and that one person's success is everybody's success. This interdependence becomes the basis for learning how to give and take cooperatively, how to sometimes put the needs of the family ahead of individual desires.

Kids Can Count on It

The previous vignette also highlights another aspect of doing things as a family that was mentioned by many of the children interviewed. This is the idea that they could count on an activity—like going to the mountains each summer—happening over and over again.

Children, especially young ones, have a great need for repetition. They will ask to have the same story told to them over and over, and if the parent should accidentally vary the content in any way, the child will probably correct it. This repetition helps children to put the world in some manageable order by providing them with an anchor on which to hang less structured activities. It helps them learn. It offers security.

The experiences that kids liked to count on were not just recreational. Sunday morning church was one event mentioned as a special time:

> We go to church almost every Sunday. It's kind of boring, really, but in a way it means a lot to have your family there with you at church.

If you are surprised that religious services are considered quality parenting by many children, you may be even more surprised that doing chores was also frequently mentioned. Jamie's comments are not unusual:

> When we wash the car, we do it all together. It's work and fun at the same time. I like helping to do something that really needs doing. It makes me feel needed.

The key to enjoying chores seems to be that the whole family, parents included, chip in. The car (or the yard or the kitchen) gets clean and a potential hassle is turned into a quality experience.

There's another benefit from doing chores together as a family. When kids feel needed, as Jamie did, when they feel that the contributions they can make to the family's welfare are important, their self-esteem improves.

"We did it all together" often included others outside the nuclear family—aunts, uncles, cousins, and grandparents.

> Some of the best times I can remember were on my grandparents' farm during Thanksgiving. There'd be a bunch of kids, cousins and all, and we'd all go upstairs in the cold house. We'd all run to the attic and jump in the bed, cover up, and just lie still until we warmed up the bed. Then we'd talk until we fell asleep. It was a lot of fun up there.

It has often been said that what children need are roots and wings. A well-defined family, one that shares many experiences of "doing it all together," can provide the roots. An extended family can increase a child's sense of belonging and connectedness, thereby strengthening these roots. However, in an age when families are spread across the country, such experiences with relatives are becoming increasingly rare. As an alternative to the traditional extended family we can develop support networks in our own communities. Through affiliations with other families with similar circumstances or interests, we can share many of the same benefits that we might with relatives.

Parents Put Kids' Needs First

> I can remember when I was about six, when we first moved here. It was summer and I didn't have any friends in my neighborhood. My mom, she quit work so she could spend a lot of time with me. We had wonderful times hopping in the pool and playing together. I know how much she loves to work because she loves to have something to do, nonstop like that, and she feels like she's accomplishing something. But she quit because she thought I was having a tough time.

We're not suggesting that parents give up their careers to be home with their families. Nor are we talking about a kind of martyrdom where kids' needs always come before parents' needs. We are saying, however, that our children often notice when we do put their needs first, even if the issues involved are not major ones. Renee remembers family outings:

> We used to go to places like Opryland and Libertyland in Memphis, and that was always fun. My dad, you know, he's real busy and he doesn't always like to go to these places. He'd rather watch football. But he would take us there and he'd ride the rides with us. My mom was afraid of them, but my dad would ride on the roller coasters and stuff. It was fun.

Renee's story underscores the importance that children place on parents' occasionally ignoring their own preferences and instead putting their kids' choices first. Many of the other stories told to us indicated that children are also aware of how busy most parents are. They notice and appreciate when parents take time out of their work to do something with them.

> When we lived in the city, my mom and stepdad took us to museums on Saturday. Sometimes we'd go just for a little while and sometimes we'd stay all day. My mom and my stepdad both work a lot on weekends, but they take time out anyway to make sure I get to do something that's really different from just sitting home and watching TV.

A few generations ago, in many families, parents did put kids' needs first—all the time. These parents often ended up feeling angry and resentful as their kids became self-centered and uncooperative. Then the pendulum swung perhaps a little too far the other way, when the "me generation" came into vogue and we learned to "look out for number one." The secret, of course, is to balance our own legitimate needs with those of our children. In any family, there should be a constant shifting of who is first and whose needs are most pressing at any particular time.

When we put this **QP** factor into practice, our attitude will communicate, "I'm choosing to do this right now because you are really important to me." The high quality of those moments together will be one of our rewards. Another may show up later, when our children better understand that they must sometimes put others' needs first.

Parents Show They Care

> Last spring I bicycled over to a field where my father was planting peanuts. I sat down and started eating the seed peanuts. My dad caught me and said, "Son, those things have been poisoned to keep the insects out. You better go tell your mom."

I bicycled home as hard as I could. When I got to the yard I was going so fast I fell and skinned my knee. My mom came out and asked me what was wrong. I was crying and told her what happened. She told me she didn't think there was enough poison on the peanuts to hurt me. She cleaned me up, took me to see the doctor, and then got me an ice-cream cone. I was scared but she made it all right.

Every child wants to feel cared for. To a young child the world can seem like a huge and dangerous place over which they have little control. Even a small and familiar peanut can suddenly precipitate a frightening crisis. Because children realize that this is the condition of their universe, they need the security of knowing that someone bigger and stronger is there to care for them.

The time you spend caring for your child makes him or her feel not only safe and secure but also special. The secret of this connection between caring and specialness is illustrated in a beautiful story by Antoine de St.-Exupéry, *The Little Prince.* In this story the little prince has a special rose. One day he leaves his home planet—and his rose—to travel about the universe. While visiting Earth, he comes upon a field of roses. Since all of the roses look just like his rose, the Little Prince thinks for a moment that his lovely rose isn't as special as he had thought. Then he has an insight. He realizes that what makes his rose special in all the universe is his caring for this one particular rose. All the times the Little Prince has watered her and weeded her and kept her safe have made her unique for him. The more he cared for her, the more special she became.

Caring for our children does make them special. Special in this sense means important, not specially privileged. All children need to learn that they must abide by the rules, take turns, and otherwise live cooperatively.

We show caring when we are empathetic to our youngsters' problems and weaknesses, resisting the urge to add to their humiliation and embarrassment:

> I've always gotten sick in the car, ever since I was born. Especially when we went to the beach. My parents were real patient with me. I mean it must have upset them but they were nice about it and didn't yell at me and stuff. They just showed they cared. So the car trips were fun instead of being awful.

We weren't surprised that kids felt cared-for when parents comforted them when they were sick or fearful. But boys and girls also expressed similar feelings when parents showed concern about their general well-being. Jeff says:

> Every night my mom made me take a bath and made sure my teeth were brushed. Then she read me and my brothers a book before we went to bed. That helped us sleep better. She was showing she cared for us.

Memories like Jeff's illustrate how children appreciate rules and routines. Despite their protestations at the time, children feel cared for when their parents make sure they do what's good for them.

Parents also show caring by helping kids with the work they have to do. Asking if we can help when a child seems overwhelmed with school work and chores will be greatly valued. That doesn't mean doing our son's arithmetic homework for him. Rather it may involve helping to organize a notebook or finding a missing paper. Allison's mom helped her in another way:

> My mom always helps me sell my Girl Scout cookies. She drives me around and waits in the car while I ring doorbells because she knows it's important to me.

Parents can be too helpful at times. Too much service and assistance teaches children to be helpless and dependent. Bail them out too often and youngsters become irresponsible.

Taking over for them communicates our lack of confidence in their abilities and lowers their self-esteem.

How, then, do we know when to help out and when to stand back? Certainly in any potentially dangerous situation we have to intervene immediately. And occasionally, when too many ill winds blow in one day, assistance can be appreciated without being expected tomorrow. But in general, it makes sense not to do things for our kids on a regular basis that they can do for themselves.

There's one final way that parents often show they care. Just as we generally pursue our own happiness, we are in a powerful position to help our children pursue theirs. Often, it's the little things that we can do that communicate our desire to see them happy—a trip to the store, a game of catch, a special lawnmower.

> I can remember my grandmother had an old lawnmower that didn't work. So my dad took all the engine parts out and made the handle my size. I liked to walk along behind him with my very own mower when he cut the grass. The other kids had little bitty plastic mowers but I had a real one. I guess my dad just liked doing things like that for me.

Sometimes youngsters feel that our main function in life is to thwart their happiness through discipline. Though certainly an important part of our role as parents, discipline works best when our children know that we care about their happiness. As we suggested in Chapter 1, the positive experiences that we share with our children become the reserve from which we can draw in times of conflict.

Kids Feel Grown-up

> Last summer my family went on a clipper ship across Lake Michigan. My mom said she'd take me to a movie on the boat

but I really wanted to stay with my dad and uncle in the lounge. Dad must have known what I was thinking because he whispered to me to stay with him so we could dance. I liked being treated like a big girl.

It's no secret kids like to pretend they're grown-up. That's why just about every preschool and kindergarten in the country has a box of dress-up clothes and a housekeeping corner where young children can assume adult roles.

In addition to providing our children with the chance to pretend, it's possible to offer them real opportunities to think and act grown-up. We can ask their opinions and preferences on matters that relate to their own care. "How early should the alarm be set so that you won't have to rush to be ready for school?" "Would you rather have the plain or mint-flavored toothpaste?" Such choices might not seem important to us as adults because the issues involved are relatively minor. To children, however, they are very meaningful, for the issue to them is one of personal power. By giving choices we give them a way to exercise control over parts of their lives that were previously controlled by their parents.

Youngsters will also feel grown-up when asked to take part in the planning that affects the whole family. We interviewed families in which children were involved in choosing the weekly menus, deciding where to go for family outings and vacations, scheduling clean-up jobs, setting up the weekly TV-viewing schedule, and solving problems between family members. *Megatrends* author John Naisbitt describes how adults cooperate best when allowed to be a part of the decision-making process; we believe the same is true for children.

Involving kids in adult activities is another way to help them feel grown-up—as Ellen's grandmother did:

I like to go to Nana's on weekends. She lets me help out around her beauty shop. I stack the colored curlers in boxes, I arrange the tubes of perm stuff on the shelves, and then I clean the

combs with some smelly liquid. I'd rather do that than play
with the box of old toys Nana keeps for me.

You don't have to have a business in your home to involve
your kids in your work. As they talk about their day during
dinner, you might share the highlights of yours. If you bring
work home, you could show the contents of your briefcase to
them. Older children, like Michael, can be invited to take
part in business discussions:

> Sometimes at night when we're sitting around the dinner table
> my father asks me what I think of something that's happening
> on his job. I like to give my opinion and it feels great that what
> I think means something to him.

Our last example of making kids feel grown-up involves
switching roles. The parent takes on what is usually the
child's job and the child does the parent's:

> My mom doesn't cook much during the week. She says my
> brother and sister and I are old enough to learn to get supper
> ready. She does the cleanup—the job we used to do, and we do
> the cooking. I cook on Tuesdays. I usually make different kinds
> of casseroles, like with sauerkraut and hot dogs. Sometimes it's
> a pain but it's fun to have everybody sit around the table wait-
> ing for me to put the food out.

Sometimes we have a tendency to wait until our kids have
"earned" the right to be treated like grown-ups before we
allow them to take part in family decisions or enjoy special
privileges or duties. In fact, it's better not to wait. When children are treated as if they are grown-up, they often act more
responsibly.

Everyone Is Relaxed

We go out to eat a lot. Last week was a holiday and we went downtown to a fancy restaurant for lunch. Dad gave the busboy some money so he would keep bringing hot French bread to our table. We all had a great time because Dad was in such a good mood.

Frankly, we were surprised to see this QP factor come up so often. It suggests that, for a lot of kids, having their parents in a good mood is the exception, not the rule. The old Norman Rockwell poster from the fifties may still have some truth for today: the boss takes out his frustrations on the father, who then takes out his frustrations on the mother, who takes hers out on the oldest kid, who dumps on the youngest child, who then kicks the dog. Perhaps the sequence has changed—it may be the mother who's yelled at by the boss—but the result is the same. When we give in to the temptation to take out our frustrations on our families, we create an atmosphere in which quality parenting is unable to thrive.

One way we can learn to relax more at home is to reject the ad slogan that says we really can "have it all." We've yet to find a way to keep our homes immaculate, cook gourmet meals, jog three miles, work eight hours, enjoy some time alone with our spouse or friends, and still have lots of time and energy left for quality parenting. For most people, each day presents a number of choices. The trick is to concentrate on those that are really relevant to family happiness and let go of the others. No one—child or adult—is going to look back on today and say, "I was really unhappy back then because there was dust on the table."

Another way to be more relaxed is to strive for improvement in our quality parenting, not perfection. Remember, what we're really advising is 10 percent more quality parenting today than yesterday, not attempting to make every family experience a four-star award-winner.

We can develop a more easygoing attitude by refusing to take things too seriously, allowing ourselves to enjoy a sense of humor, and not overreacting to every little transgression on our kids' part. It takes only a little flexibility to take unexpected inconveniences in stride, rather than turning them into crises:

> We were on a family camping trip—hiking through the mountains with backpacks and tents and things. It started to rain, and everyone was disappointed. We were too far to turn back but we still had three or four hours of hiking left before we reached the campsite. So we took out our ponchos and kept on sloshing. Dad started a chorus of "Singing in the Rain," and pretty soon we were singing all the "rain" songs we know. It turned out to be one of the best trips we ever took. In fact, a family motto came out of it. Someone would yell, "What makes for a good trip?" and everyone else would yell back, "Rain."

Unfortunately, you may not find a silver lining in every cloud. Sometimes the best strategy is to just cut your losses and go on to something else. Try not to "beat a dead horse," dwelling on some misfortune or some trouble a child has been in. Deal with the situation, make sure everyone understands what's happened, and move on.

For many of the girls and boys in our study, having parents relaxed made them feel safe and secure. Here's how Susan describes dinner preparations in her family:

> I love our cookouts. Everyone is relaxed and easygoing. Before the food is ready I go in and out of the house getting stuff for the picnic table. Mom and Dad don't get uptight and criticize or yell at us when we're outside like they do sometimes in the house.

We are not suggesting that we must be in a good mood 100 percent of the time. We know that's not possible. When we do find ourselves feeling out-of-sorts, however, we can go slowly and not push for too much contact. There's nothing wrong with saying, "Something happened at work today that's put me in a really bad mood. I'm going to sulk in the bathtub for a while and get rid of my crabbiness." Later, when we're more relaxed, we can look for opportunities for quality experiences.

Parents Make It Fun

> We have tons of trees in our yard. Once a week, in October, we'd all have to go out to rake leaves. After a while it gets boring. Then my dad would stop and throw us in a big pile of leaves. That was like a break from work and everything and it was fun.

If fun is a universal language, then childhood is it's native tongue. When we share enjoyable activities with our children, relationships are strengthened and barriers to communication removed. In fact, because this QP factor came up over and over again in our interviews, we believe that it is one of the surest ingredients for quality parenting.

One way to make things fun is to do the unexpected. By providing a twist in the usual routine, an unpleasant task can be turned into an enjoyable event. Eating leftovers is not something most families eagerly anticipate, yet one creative family managed to turn it into a favorite weekly event:

> Every Sunday afternoon we have a picnic inside the house. Mom spreads our old camping blanket on the dining-room floor. She serves all the leftovers in the refrigerator that she wants to get rid of. Sometimes the mixtures we eat are real weird but nobody much minds. We use paper plates and plastic forks just like on a real picnic. Dad teases Mom about how next week he's going to bring some ants so we'll really think we're outside.

Since most people enjoy a friendly challenge, we can make things fun by turning everyday happenings into a game. The fun is spoiled, however, when the competition becomes too intense. In fact, in some of the best games, family members team up against the clock or the job at hand rather than against each other. For example, the Pushkin family was able to turn getting dressed for school into *Beat the Clock:*

> I used to have trouble getting ready for school. Mom yelled a lot and Dad threatened not to let me watch TV if I didn't hurry up. Then they surprised me with a little box wrapped with a big blue bow. I was so excited because it wasn't my birthday or anything. Inside was a kitchen timer and a note that said, "Congratulations. You have just been selected as a contestant on *Beat the Clock.* Each morning your parents will set the timer for thirty minutes when they wake you up. If you are dressed and downstairs before the timer goes off, you win the game." For my prize sometimes I get a sticker or an extra-big hug.

Some parents make it fun by making it funny. One mother found a humorous cure for deafness to parents. Instead of resorting to the usual disciplinary tactics, when she wanted her children's attention she simply talked to them in a voice with a funny accent. This mom could imitate a Texas cowboy, a southern belle, a squawking parrot, even a modern computer.

Speaking in a monotone, this computer delivered an endless supply of messages to kids in the family:

> "Now . . . is . . . the . . . time . . . for . . . din . . . ner. Please . . . wash . . . all . . . hands . . . and . . . dir . . . ty . . . fa . . . ces . . . be . . . fore . . . you . . . sit . . . down."

Another way we can have fun with our children is to get into the childlike part of our own personality and do things that generally only kids do. Margo's mother surprised her one winter:

Last year there was one of those big snows where they closed down the schools for a couple of days. We have a big hill in our backyard that all the kids would go down on their sleds. My mother came out to check to see how things were going. She surprised me by asking for a turn. She got on the sled and I got behind her. We went down this hill real fast and were laughing our heads off.

When thinking about this QP factor, it's important to keep in mind the difference between acting *childlike* and acting *childish*. The *Oxford American Dictionary* defines *childlike* as having "the good qualities of a child, simple and innocent." *Childish,* on the other hand, suggests an "immature, misbehaving quality." In Lester's story below, his father acts childish rather than childlike:

We have a lot of fun at suppertime. Dad likes to act silly. He makes pyramids out of the salad dressing bottles. Sometimes he puts his plate on top of Mom's glass. I like the food fights the best. One night Mom had just bought some new curtains for the kitchen window. My dad picked up a spoon of baked beans and plopped them on my sister's plate. She scooped them up and put them back on Dad's plate. Then he took the spoon and made a sling out of it with the beans. His aim was bad and it ended up with beans all over Mom's new curtains.

Lester clearly enjoyed these dinnertimes, but just because kids think something is fun isn't reason enough to continue. The fun was at someone else's expense—Mom's. Acting childish in ways that are socially unacceptable is just plain setting a bad example.

Even acting childlike has certain limits. A camp director once said that the difference between the counselors and the campers was that the counselor played with one eye on the clock. The parent must know where the limits are and when to begin acting like an adult again.

When taken as a whole, these QP factors offer an excellent view of quality parenting as seen through the eyes of children. We will build on this understanding in the chapters that follow as we explore the skills and activities that make quality parenting happen.

Chapter 3

SHARING

There is an art to quality parenting, and like any art, it will flourish best if we develop some skills. In analyzing our research, we saw over and over again that four specific skills form the bedrock of quality parenting. These skills are sharing, encouraging, playing, and teaching—the subjects of this chapter and the following chapters. Sharing, the skill we will discuss first, provides a closeness between parents and children and helps our kids understand their own feelings.

Close Encounters

A college student once posted a quote on his wall as a reminder to himself and his roommate. It simply said, "Shared joy is double joy." We also know that "misery loves company." In other words, whether happy or sad, most people want to have someone with whom to share their experiences.

Real sharing involves revealing our thoughts and feelings to another human being. It can be one of the most satisfying experiences in our lives. Yet we often hold back because we feel we have to protect ourselves. When we share who we really are, we become vulnerable. We risk being criticized, ridiculed, looked down upon, or even physically harmed. We fear that if others really knew us, they might not like us, and would reject us. So instead of opening up, we usually play it safe and reveal only superficial information about ourselves—at the same time we long to share more deeply.

Though teenagers are often busy carving out private psychological space for themselves, most children want to share with us. Stories like the following came up frequently in the interviews:

> My mother picks me up after school every day. We have a long ride home and we just talk. It's a special time because I can tell her things about the day and she really cares.

What makes it possible for children to trust us enough to share themselves? To approach us with problems? To share their dreams, their hurts? Part of the answer lies in our ability to protect them. Just as we often hold back out of fear of being hurt or rejected, our children also learn that sharing can be risky. If what they tell us is sure to result in discipline or will not be taken seriously or kept private, our kids will be wary. However, if they can trust that we will accept them once we know them, and if we can develop the skills that promote sharing, they will eagerly take the risk.

To get an idea of how much your child has been sharing with you, see how many of the following questions you can answer:

1. What are your child's three biggest fears?

2. Who is your child's best friend?

3. What are his or her three favorite activities?

4. Who is your child's favorite teacher of all time? What does your child like about that teacher?

5. Who is your child's least-favorite teacher of all time? What does he or she dislike about that teacher?

6. How does your child wish he or she were different?

7. What does your child like best about you?

8. How do they wish that you were different?

It's unlikely that we can answer all of these questions because these are not the areas where we usually focus our conversations. It's as if we and our children are mountains resting underwater on the ocean floor and extending up through the surface and into the sky. Above the surface, the mountain peaks are distant from each other. On the ocean floor, they actually touch. Above the water are our day-to-day encounters. They are important in their own right, but if we communicate only above the surface, we miss out on the joys of deeper sharing, the close encounters in which we might truly touch one another.

These close encounters—the sharing of thoughts, feelings, goals, dreams, and experiences—require that we not only listen to our children, but also disclose parts of ourselves. In the first part of this chapter, we will look at those skills that enable us to focus on our children better. Then we'll look at how we can help our children know us better.

Skills to Help You Focus on Your Child

Have you ever noticed that few people really listen? We receive information passively, without paying full attention, or using the full range of our senses. When we allow ourselves to become distracted by such interruptions as the TV, barking dogs, the newspaper, or the phone, it may seem that we are trying to carry on a conversation in a three-ring circus.

In fact, a popular comic strip called *The Family Circus* recently showed a little boy talking to his father, who was distracted by his newspaper and the TV. "You hafta listen to me with your eyes, Daddy," said the boy. "Not just your ears."

The best listening requires the focus of our eyes as well as our ears because a lot of information is communicated non-verbally, by facial expressions and body language. Without full concentration, we are bound to miss a great deal.

The type of listening that promotes sharing cannot be done while we are thinking of other things. When possible, it is best to completely stop what we are doing and give our child undivided attention. At other times, even though our hands may be busy with a routine job, packing a briefcase or loading the dishwasher, we can still focus most of our attention on our child. We might even be working together on a task as we talk. For some children, the lack of direct eye contact and the informality of doing a job together actually makes it easier to say what's on their mind. Later, they may feel comfortable in continuing the conversation eye-to-eye. In fact, picking the right time, is an important element in learning to share. There are times when it is not practical to begin an in-depth conversation at all. If other people are walking in and out of the room or if the school bus is about to arrive, the best choice may be to make a date to talk later.

Once you have made time to fully listen to what your child has to share, the second step is to keep listening. This may sound redundant, but one of the mistakes parents make most frequently is to jump in prematurely with advice or otherwise take over the conversation. We may have a solution to a problem on the tip of our tongue, or the wisdom of the ages burning in our heart to be shared, but if we give in to the temptation to blurt it out prematurely, it will likely fall on deaf ears, and cut off further communication. As one mother put it, "We have two ears and one mouth, so we ought to listen twice as much as we talk."

Listening for Feelings

Many people listen to the content of a story, barely noticing the feelings beneath, yet these feelings play an important part in communication. When people know that their feelings have been understood, they experience a strong sense of relief. Such sharing can bring two people closer together, and can set the stage for problem-solving or productive work or joyful play.

Listening for feelings requires an understanding of the vocabulary of emotion. Unfortunately, most of us have a limited vocabulary when it comes to feelings. We know the basic emotions: anger, sadness, joy, happiness, disgust, and hurt. When we search for subtle variations, however, we often become tongue-tied. For example, how many shades of anger can you name? There is irritation, annoyance, defiance, rebellion, frustration, resentment, rancor, and rage, to list a few. By adding a modifier, we can create more variations. Are you "annoyed" or "fairly annoyed"? Are you "enraged" (which may mean that I'm in trouble) or are you "totally enraged" (which may mean that I should duck)? Giving names to feelings increases our awareness of the varieties of emotion, and our means for talking about feelings with our children.

Children, who are usually very poor at expressing their feelings in words, will often express them through tone of voice or behavior. When the feelings are negative, this can mean misbehavior or temper tantrums. It may help in dealing with such "misbehavior" to simply ask, "What is my child really feeling right now?"

A famous internist once said that to be a good doctor, one must "see with the patient's eyes, hear with his ears, and feel with his heart." This same willingness to empathize is important in sharing feelings with our children. What does it feel like to be a five-year-old on the way to school for the first time? Or a ten-year-old who just received a low grade on an important test? Or a fifteen-year-old who is being pressured by friends to use drugs? By tuning in fully to the clues that our children give—their facial expressions, body language, tone of voice, and other behavior—we can strengthen our ability to hear the feelings our children have not learned to put into words.

Responding to Feelings

Once we have listened for the feelings behind our children's words, we can respond in a way that communicates understanding. Let's look at an example:

> Megan: Mommy, would you please ask Joel to stay out of my room?
> Mother: It sounds like you're pretty irritated with your brother.
> Megan: Yeah. He keeps getting into my things.
> Mother: I guess you're worried that he might damage something
> Megan: Yeah. Last time he spilled lotion all over my pink sweater.
> Mother: I know, you were furious at him.

The mother in this example uses two important responding skills. First, she is patient. Instead of trying to solve the problem immediately, she continues to focus on her daughter's underlying feelings. Second, when she responds to those feelings, she does so tentatively, using such phrases as "it sounds like" and "I guess" to allow the child room to decide for herself what she is actually feeling. We don't want our kids to get the idea that we are trying to read their minds or that we know it all. Instead, we are simply taking a guess at what they are feeling. If the mother had been off target,

Megan could easily have corrected her tentative guesses, with no harm done to the communication. For example:

> Mother: It sounds like you are pretty irritated with your brother.
> Megan: Irritated, nothing! I'm about to kill him!
> Mother: Wow! You're really furious, aren't you?

Although the mother undershot the emotion on her first try, she was easily able to correct herself with a little feedback from her daughter. When a parent does respond with the correct "feeling word," an interesting thing usually happens. The child nods her head up and down, she says yes, and she begins to elaborate. She may even express the emotion more deeply. For instance, if you name sadness, tears may well up; if you touch anger, the child's voice may become louder and her face red. In effect, you will have given permission to the child to feel and express whatever it is that she is experiencing.

Ironically, we often avoid naming our children's feelings because we fear that our words will make them lose control. For example, let's say that we see our child looking sad, and we respond by saying, "You sure look unhappy." If our child then bursts into tears, sobbing uncontrollably, we may feel that we have just made a bad situation worse. Actually, the opposite is true. Almost all mental health experts agree that it is much better to express strong feelings than to keep them inside, because hidden feelings will eventually make themselves known in one way or another. We have already mentioned how they may find an outlet through misbehavior, but such feelings may also come out in the form of stomachaches, headaches, or other physical problems, as well as in school and learning problems.

It's important to accept all our children's feelings, even the ugly ones. This is the only way they will feel safe enough to put their feelings into words. Criticizing or punishing a negative feeling does not make it go away. In fact, it is more likely to strengthen it. This does not mean we accept *behavior* that is destructive or unkind. It is the feelings we are dealing with here. When we offer a calm presence to help a child get these feelings into the open, he or she will usually regain control and be willing to look for constructive ways to handle the problem.

Listen for the Real Meaning

Children may have difficulty talking about their feelings or, when they do speak, they may not express their true thoughts. Instead, they will speak in a sort of code, giving us clues about their real concerns and leaving it up to us to decipher their message. Sometimes they are just beating around the bush. They may be unable to pinpoint exactly what is bothering them or what they want to say. At other times they are not sure if their thoughts or concerns are okay, so they test the water with seemingly unimportant questions. For example:

> Benjamin: Dad, how many divorces are there each year?
> Father: I don't know, son. Do you mean in the U.S. or here in Seattle?
> Benjamin: I don't know. Here, I guess.
> Father: Well, let's see. The national average is about forty percent. I imagine Seattle is pretty close to that. So we'd have to find out how many married couples there are here. Do you want to go to the library, so we can look it up?
> Benjamin: Nah, that's okay. I was just wondering.

What was Benjamin "just wondering"? Dad took his question literally and assumed that he was wondering about statistics. But if we look beneath the overt question, we might find that Benjamin was wondering about something much more personal. He may have been wondering if his parents were going to get divorced. If so, it's understandable that he lost interest when his father suggested a trip to the library. After all, the librarian is not likely to have the information he seeks.

By listening for the real messages behind our children's words, we can help them clarify their thoughts and find answers for their real concerns. For example, let's suppose that your son says to you one morning, "I don't want to go to school today; I have a stomachache." If you take this message at face value, you might give him some Pepto Bismol, a kind word, and send him on his way. If you are a soft touch, you might let him spend the day at home. Or you might even take him to the doctor.

But if you were to talk further with your child while listening for the real meaning, you might find that there is something about going to school that worries him. Children use "stomachaches" to cover up hidden messages. Sometimes they are saying, "I'm afraid of getting beat up on the bus," or "I'm not prepared for my history test," or "I did something really stupid yesterday and I don't want to face the other kids." Of course, sometimes a stomachache is just a stomachache, but when there is more to it, what good will the Pepto Bismol really do?

We can help uncover the underlying meaning by becoming a detective and listening for our child's feelings. In this example, if we heard the child's fear beneath the complaint of stomachache, we would be well on the way to breaking the case. We could ask probing questions. "What's going on in school today? You sound worried." When asked with a sympathetic and caring tone, such questions make it safe for our children to share what's really bothering them. However, if we ask like an investigator trying to break a suspect, or if our attitude is critical rather than supporting, we might as well

pour the Pepto Bismol. They are not going to tell to us anything.

Responding to the Real Meaning

Once we have an idea of the real meaning of a child's messages, we can gently shift the conversation in that direction.
Again, we want to respond to the feelings as well as the
content. Let's take another look at our divorce example.

> Benjamin: Dad, how many divorces are there each year?
> Father: Quite a few, I'm afraid.
> Benjamin: Well, why do so many people get divorced? I think
> it's stupid.
> Father: You sound kind of sad about that.
> Benjamin: Yeah, well, Jeremy's parents just told him they were
> getting a divorce.
> Father: I see. That must be pretty tough on Jeremy.
> Benjamin: Uh-huh. He doesn't even know where he'll live now.
> Father: That's kind of scary, isn't it?
> Benjamin: Uh-huh.
> Father: Are you worried that Mom and I might get divorced
> some day?
> Benjamin: Well, you do fight a lot.

The father in this example did a good job with his detective work. Benjamin was not interested in statistics, he was
interested in probability, namely, the probability that his
own parents might divorce. Once the father had correctly
identified the real meaning behind his son's question, he
could continue to help Ben express his feelings about the
subject. Then, he could look for opportunities to reassure
him or otherwise offer new information. Together, parents
and children can often come up with innovative solutions to
thorny problems, and create quality encounters in the process.

Sharing Yourself with Your Child

Our focus so far has been on the skills that will enable our children to share more of themselves with us, but as we discussed earlier, the potential for quality parenting is much greater when the parents also are willing to reveal themselves. Parents are sometimes reticent about the less flattering sides of themselves because they want their children to see their "good side." Therefore they carefully conceal anything negative. For example, we may believe that we must always appear brave and in control for our children to feel secure.

We do not believe that seeing some of their parents' vulnerable side will cause youngsters harm. On the contrary, it can be very helpful. One teenager told us that when he was sixteen, he was going through some old papers in a trunk and found a French test that his father had failed. The teen described his feeling as "uplifting." "For the first time in my life, I had the feeling that I could live up to the standard he had set with all his accomplishments."

Some parents have trouble talking to their children about their own good points. We may feel that it's our job to listen to our kids' triumphs and dreams, not to speak about ours. In trying not to boast we keep our children from getting to know a side of us that they might value. Sometimes we can be as "stingy" in sharing our good attributes with our kids as our foibles.

We are not suggesting that we make our children our confidants or best friends. The A-to-Z sharing that is appropriate between two adults is more than a child should have to handle. When deciding what to share, it helps to keep in mind the child's age and level of maturity. Obviously, we don't want to speak in front of our children about the details of a neighbor's divorce, for example, or about other matters that are clearly not their business.

It also is not a good idea to use stories about our own lives to manipulate rather than support. Children don't want to hear about the proverbial five miles we had to walk through snow and ice to get to school—especially if our motive is to put them down for complaining about having to ride the school bus. Guilt trips, attempts to gain sympathy, and stories designed to pressure a child into doing things our way usually backfire.

One of the most useful purposes of self-disclosure is to offer support to a child when he or she is down. By responding first to the child's feeling, then by sharing a similar experience from our own lives, we can let the child know that he or she can survive the trauma:

> Mother: What's the matter, sweetheart? You look as if the world just ended.
> Latrice: I hate Charlene. She invited everybody to her party but me.
> Mother: Oh, honey. I know that really hurts because I can remember the same thing.
> Latrice: Huh? What do you mean?
> Mother: Well, one time when I was just a little older than you are right now, there was this girl named Aretha. She didn't like me too much. Well, actually that's not exactly right. To be honest, she hated my guts.
> Latrice: Why?
> Mother: I don't know. It was probably kind of silly, but we just didn't like each other. We were always putting each other down and stuff. Well, she invited some of the kids up to the lake to go swimming, including a boy that I really liked. Needless to say, she didn't invite yours truly.
> Latrice: Were you mad?
> Mother: Mad? Honey, I wanted to kill her! Her up at the lake with Robert and the others, and me stuck at home. I thought I would die.

By disclosing a similar experience of her own, this mother has, in effect, joined Latrice in her misery. Human nature being what it is, when disaster strikes, most of us feel better if we have some company. This mother's good-natured recalling of her own story also indicates that she got over it. This communicates to Latrice that she too will get over her bad feelings. If her mother just said, "You'll get over it," Latrice would probably feel that she was taken for granted, and that her mother didn't really understand. Finally, her mother's self-disclosure validates Latrice's feelings. It says that it's okay to feel angry and hurt over this; you needn't compound your bad feelings by feeling bad about feeling bad. All of this adds up to a very supportive interaction.

You don't have to refer to your childhood to share yourself. Many situations offer rich material. For example, Latrice's mother might have told about the time when some of her co-workers went to lunch at a special restaurant and didn't invite her.

Another purpose of self-disclosure is to show the child that there are various ways to handle difficult situations. Children are often myopic when it comes to problem-solving. With few life experiences to draw upon, they may see only one or two of the many options that exist. We can help broaden their perspective by lending them some of our life experiences. Because the subtle effect of a shared story is much less threatening than direct advice, children are more open to thinking about the alternatives implied.

Latrice: What did you do?
Mother: Well, I felt sorry for myself for a little while. I moped around the house until I realized I was doing exactly what she wanted me to—being miserable.
Latrice: So what did you do?
Mother: I decided that I had to get out of the house. So I made about six calls, and I finally found someone who wanted to go to a movie with me and we had a really good time.
Latrice: What happened to Aretha?
Mother: Well, when the other kids found out that she had purposely left me out, they were pretty mad at her. It made her look bad, not me.

Explaining what we did in a similar situation opens up possibilities for our children, but we don't want to give them the impression that we expect them to handle things the same way, or that we have all the answers. Allowing children to make decisions for themselves helps build their self-confidence, independence, and sense of responsibility and also shows that we respect them.

Sharing particularly meaningful experiences is another important way to create an emotional connection with our children. When we share something that has touched us, we invite our children deeper into our own lives. These moments are among the most beautiful, and rare, that a parent and child can experience.

> Father: Richard, honey, want to see something funny? I was just going through these old photos that Grandpa gave us after Grandma died.
> Richard: Was that really you? You look like a hippy.
> Father: Well, I was pretty hip, but I wasn't a real hippy.
> Richard: Is this you when you were a little boy?
> Father: Let me see. Yeah, that was taken on a family vacation. We were at a national park and had just hiked to the waterfall. I remember Mom and I hiked together while Dad and your uncle Ken went up ahead. She taught me an army chant that went, "Your left, your left. You had a good job but you left. You left your wife and fourteen kids without a can of gingerbread, did you do right? Your right, your right. You had a good job, but you left. You left, you left . . ." We kept singing it over and over marching through the woods holding hands. She was so full of fun and spirit back then. I wish you could have known her before she got sick.
> Richard: I wish I could too. . . . Dad? Do you miss Grandma very much?
> Father: Sometimes I do. Like now, when I think about all the good times we had together and how much time she took teaching me things. I guess that's what's left of us after we die—the memories people keep in their hearts . . .
> Richard: Dad? Will you teach me how to do that army march?

Chapter 4

ENCOURAGING

For children to gain confidence in themselves and to flourish, they need from their parents an essential ingredient of quality parenting—encouragement. And, most definitely, they don't need its opposite—discouragement.

To put it another way, we must avoid robbing our children of their courage and must try to give them the heart to be the best they can.

Catch 'em Being Good

My daughter's class went to see a play at the performing arts center and the next day her teacher called me and said, "I'd like to talk to you about your daughter." I asked her what she had done now, and her teacher told me that Rachel's helpfulness had made the entire trip go better for everyone. I thanked her for calling and hung up. I couldn't believe it, but I felt terrific, so I told my daughter what her teacher said. She also felt terrific—I could see by her face how much that call had meant to her.

By encouraging her daughter with this story, this mother accomplished two goals. First, she built on Rachel's willingness to cooperate. When we focus our attention on our children's positive behavior and let them know we appreciate what they have done, their response is usually to do more of the same in the future. Our words become a powerful motivator. In this example, by "catching her" being helpful, the teacher and mother have teamed up to foster more of this desirable behavior.

Second, when she took the time to share the teacher's compliments with her daughter, this mother created a quality interaction between the two of them. When we acknowledge our child's positive actions, no matter how minor, we strengthen the connection that exists between the two of us.

We don't have to wait until the teacher calls to catch our child being good. Dozens of opportunities present themselves daily. Unfortunately, we often fail to notice the positive things our children do. Most of us tend to take the good for granted and focus on what is wrong. For example, we can walk into a bedroom and be totally unaware of the well-made bed and the neatly folded clothes. All we see are the dishes piled up on the desk from last night's snack. There are, of course, times you will have to correct your child, but you might also look for and comment on what he or she is doing well.

There is another reason why parents sometimes ignore the positive. Imagine your four-year-old happily playing with blocks. How likely is it that you would interrupt to say, "That's an interesting building you're making" or "I like the way you can play on your own while I'm getting dinner ready." Most parents believe that if they say anything at this point, disaster will strike, and a well-behaved little boy will suddenly turn into the incredible hulk. So they breathe a sigh of relief and go about their business, missing a golden opportunity to catch 'em being good.

Sometimes parents wonder why they should have to compliment children for behavior that is expected. Shouldn't appreciation be reserved for the extraordinary? It may seem strange, but reserving our comments for special moments is like serving food only on holidays. Encouragement is the child's basic diet. It is daily sustenance, building a base of courage and self-esteem from which extraordinary things can grow.

The following experiment was carried out on a rifle range. A marksman was blindfolded, pointed in the direction of the target, and given ten shots. As you can imagine, his tenth shot was no closer to the bull's-eye than the first. He had not improved. Another marksman also was blindfolded, pointed in the direction of the target, and given ten shots. But after each shot, the second man was told where the bullet had hit—for example, "High right." This feedback enabled him to improve his aim and eventually to zero in on the bull's-eye. Once he hit the mark, a simple "Bull's-eye" was all the encouragement he needed to maintain his accuracy.

Commenting on our children's positive behavior can also help them improve their aim. For example, let's say that you want to instill the value of honesty in your child. Perhaps he has lied to you about something very important, like taking money from your wallet. You might consider honesty under such circumstances a "bull's-eye." What you want to do—after sharing your feelings about honesty and listening to his—is to catch him being honest, and to offer your appreciation. You might look for small chances, like asking him if he has washed his hands before dinner. If he says no, you have an opportunity to say, "I appreciate your honesty; please go wash them. We'll be waiting for you." You can ask him to play a board game with you, then catch him playing fairly, and say something like, "It's fun to play with you when you play fair." Not only are you teaching honesty, but you are enjoying yourself in the process.

Showing Confidence

> My five-year-old son was showing me how he could swim in
> the shallow end of the pool. A little later I carried him out
> into the deeper end, well over his head. I asked him if he
> wanted to try swimming from the middle of the pool over to
> the side, a distance he could clearly make. Because it was
> over his head, he was frightened and said no. I told him that
> I was pretty sure he could make it and that I would swim
> along next to him. If he had any trouble he could reach out
> and grab me. We swam side by side to the edge of the pool
> with no trouble. He was very proud of his accomplishment.

This father encouraged his son to expand his limits. His
confidence, plus his willingness to lend a hand if needed,
enabled his son to overcome a fear, and develop his self-
confidence in the process.

The prototype of showing confidence is the way we teach
babies to walk. We kneel down to their level and with supportive words and outstretched hands entice them to take
that first step. "You can do it." "Come to Daddy." "Atta girl."
These are statements that communicate confidence in the
child's ability to master the task. It would be foolish to expect
him or her to walk across the entire room all at once. Instead,
we acknowledge step-by-step progress, thereby motivating
the child to persevere.

There are many creative ways to show confidence in our
children. For example, although it's no great compliment
always to be asked to take out the garbage, asking a child to
help to stain a new door or to prepare a simple casserole does
acknowledge his or her ability to handle responsibility. We
can grant certain privileges before being asked to do so—a
later bedtime, a personal house key, or permission to take the
city bus or subway alone. We can ask for our children's opinions, thereby encouraging them to think about life's problems and formulate their ideas. And we can develop a "you

can do it" attitude. Even when they fall short, we can let our kids know we believe that with more practice or a little persistence, they can succeed.

There is an obvious difference between showing confidence and expecting more from children than they can realistically accomplish. In the last vignette, for example, if the child had just recently learned to swim, the father would have been expecting too much, with failure a likely result. To avoid pushing children too far too fast, we can encourage them to move forward in small steps.

Astute observation and judgment as well as the skills of sharing will help us decipher the particular child's code and tune in to the his or her ability. Once a child is succeeding, we must guard against bringing progress to a halt by expecting perfection. When we refuse to tolerate any mistakes or failure, we undermine confidence.

Frequently, rescuing a child from potentially difficult situations is another way we show a lack of confidence. We aren't suggesting that we should avoid taking immediate action if a child's life is in danger. What we as parents want to guard against, however, is taking over only because we feel that we can solve the problem quicker and better ourselves.

Dr. Haim Ginott used to tell the story of a father and son in an ice-cream shop. The son wanted to carry his own cone, but the father assured him, "You're too little; you'll spill it." The son persisted, and the father gave in with the admonishment "Okay, but you'll spill it." Of course, the son spilled the cone.

Although this father did not actually take over, what he did was to convince his son that he couldn't handle the situation on his own. The father undermined the child's confidence enough to create the pressure that caused the mishap. When we begin a sentence with the word "Don't" (as in "Don't spill it"), we communicate that we really expect the child to make a mistake.

Many parents have found it more helpful to offer support rather than to rescue. The "ice-cream father" might have turned a self-fulfilling prophecy into a quality experience:

"I want to carry my own cone."

"Okay, I think you can do it. . . . Just take it slowly, and keep your eye on the cone. Here, let me get the chair for you. . . . Nice job!"

Cheerleading

My son had very few early successes in school. He learned to read and write later than most kids his age. To say he didn't get along with his teachers is an understatement. His first major success came during second grade, when he spent hours in the art room making pictures on paper plates with lines and dots. He used only red and purple paints, but he composed dozens of these designs—and no two were alike. His persistence was amazing. The picture-plates were hung for display in the hall and then, to top it off, parents, teachers, and students were invited to Davey's opening. Of course his dad and I were right there with the biggest smiles you've ever seen.

The mother and father in this vignette attended the art opening as cheerleaders. Parental cheerleaders are there on the sidelines, urging the team on, and cheering every point scored. They are in the audience, applauding their eight-year-old's debut on stage; xeroxing reprints of the newspaper article about a Little League victory; quoting a teenager—in his presence—about his views on some political question.

Cheerleading has two specific goals. First, when a child is doing well, we accentuate the positive feelings by cheering and getting others to join in. Conversely, when our child does poorly, we try, by encouragement, to motivate persistence in improvement. Either way, we want our children to know that we are behind them 100 percent.

When we are cheerleading at an event, sitting in the stands

or in the audience, we may not be interacting with our child, but our presence is felt nevertheless. Afterward, we can talk and reminisce about the experience. Photographs of the event can help us relive these quality moments later.

Parental cheerleaders want their children to be the best that they can be. This means giving them permission to be either different from or more successful than their parents. Just as real cheerleaders do not compete with the team, we do not want to compete with our children. Instead, we want to give the message "I'm pulling for you. I'm happy when you succeed. You're the star."

For the moment, let's imagine a ten-year-old who just made an A in math for the first time in his life. He runs all the way home from school to show his parents, and as he enthusiastically tells them about his triumph, their only response is a blasé "Very good, dear." How would he feel?

Such a lack of appropriate enthusiasm, the opposite of cheerleading, is tremendously discouraging. It's even worse when a parent actually rains on the child's parade. Imagine how the boy might feel if his parents had responded, "Don't get on your high horse. You know that teacher isn't very hard. Wait until next year when you're in fifth grade."

Another way parents show lack of interest is by not being there—either physically or psychologically. It is not realistic to expect that we will be able to attend every important event in our child's life. If, however, we are consistently absent, and if our child takes our absence as meaning we did not care enough (we were too tired, had a party or ball game to go to, or just didn't feel up to it), then discouragement and resentment will undermine the experience.

When an important obligation does keep us away physically, we can still be there psychologically. We can call before the event to wish our child good luck (or "break a leg"), and let him or her know that we wish we could be there. Afterward we might call to offer congratulations, and to hear all about it. For really special occasions, we might even send flowers.

Some of the most creative and achieving adults we know got that way because their parents were generous with appreciation and applause. Their parents thought they were wonderful, and so they turned out to be—predictably.

Accepting Your Child

When I was ten I did something really stupid. A friend and me were in Bryant's—it's a department store—and we took some of those little matchbox cars. I don't know why we did it—I guess to see if we could get away with it—but we got caught by the store detective and he called our parents. I felt awful and was scared they'd throw a fit, but they stayed real calm. All they did was make me do a research report on stealing, but I think that's because they could see how bad I felt. My friend wasn't so lucky. His parents almost killed him.

Accepting our children, even when we do not approve of their behavior, is a real challenge. It's also a way for parents to help children learn from their mistakes, and make it through such crises as shoplifting. Acceptance is an attitude that communicates: "You're my child, and I'm glad of it, regardless of anything you might do, say, feel, or think. I might take issue with you over any of those things, but I still want you to know that I care about you and will stick with you."

Children shouldn't have to earn their parents' acceptance. Rather, it should be the one free gift that is each child's birthright. Without this acceptance, the foundation upon which their lives are built is one of doubt and insecurity. If children are accepted only when they succeed or behave the way their parents want, they never develop the feeling that they are loved and valued for themselves.

Misconceptions about parent-child relationships interfere with our ability to accept our children. We may believe that children are here to be a credit to their parents, or that they should attain the goals we set and failed to reach ourselves. Sometimes parents think that unconditional acceptance of children will lead them to misbehave. In fact, the opposite is true. Children bloom in an accepting environment.

Perhaps most difficult of all is to recognize that right now, just as they are—with all their bad habits and other imperfections—our children are worthy of our acceptance. It is hard not to confuse the deed with the doer. When children do well, it's easy to accept them. When they do poorly, particularly when they misbehave, it is easy to reject them. Either way, children come to believe that they are only the sum of their deeds. They feel that what is missing is the "real person," the essence of the child that lies beneath all his or her behavior, good and bad.

When children misbehave, it's important to focus our discipline on their behavior, rather than their character or personality. We can let our children know that it is only their behavior that is objectionable when we discipline them. Withdrawing love—and thereby acceptance—is a very destructive method of discipline. Labeling a child is equally problematic. For example, rather than saying, "You're selfish," we can focus on the behavior and say, "You're acting selfishly." We might even add a firm but friendly "Please share." If a child's behavior is such that we do not want to be around him or her at the moment, we can still communicate acceptance. Rather than giving the child the icy silent treatment, we might say something like "When you refuse to play quietly when I've asked you to, I feel very irritated because I can't relax. Please go play in your room until you can play quietly in here."

A final pitfall on the road to acceptance, and one often waiting for parents who are high achievers, is rejecting the child when he or she fails. The rejection may be subtle—an expression that communicates "You let us down"—but the message is clear: "If you want us to accept you, live up to our expectations."

It is particularly when children experience failure (and a B for a child aiming for an A may feel like a failure) that they need our acceptance most. This is a good time to use the sharing skills discussed in Chapter 3.

Keep in mind that children are usually able to read our attitudes through nuances in our behavior. A facial expression or change in tone or movement will often belie what we are saying.

Stimulating Independence

> The first time I was allowed to ride the bus, I was thirteen and had just gotten a job selling Cokes at the college football games. My parents let me take the bus to the stadium where all the other kids who were working there were. It was like going to work. It was the first money I ever earned.

Stimulating independence in a child may, at first glance, seem to run counter to the close psychological contact that we have stressed thus far as the sine qua non of quality parenting. This young teen going off to sell Cokes is not sharing an intimate moment with his parents. But there is a connection.

Developing independence—the ability to take care of oneself—is really the fundamental task of childhood. It is a process that culminates when the child eventually leaves home. If the child has reached psychological as well as physical independence, then he or she will be able to move into an adult-to-adult relationship with his or her parents in which they maintain closeness and continue to share warm experiences.

When children remain dependent upon their parents, this

separation and subsequent re-connection cannot occur. Instead, the dependency often creates hostility. Anger and resentment about control cause the relationship to deteriorate into a continuing struggle for power.

We can help children develop independence by taking the time to teach them life skills. We all begin by helping our children learn to walk, talk, eat, dress, and use the toilet. We continue with skills like cooking, cleaning, and driving. We also want to teach social skills, such as behaving considerately, playing fairly, working productively, and respecting others. Such training requires time and energy, and ironically, one of our goals as parents is to do it so well that we eventually work ourselves out of a job. Of course, while we're teaching we have another rich opportunity for quality contact with our kids.

As we've discussed, a good rule of thumb in parenting is to avoid doing on a regular basis what our children can do for themselves. When we do too much and pamper them, kids become dependent, helpless, and spoiled, and we waste precious time and energy that could be better used elsewhere. We also want to guard against the tendency to take over our children's tasks because we can do them better and faster. The time spent teaching children now, and the patience to let them handle the job, will save time later.

Showing Respect

The thing that I remember most about my dad was that he never talked down to us. Even when we were kids, he used to talk to us like we had good sense or something. Like one time when I was real little, four or five or so, and he caught me using my new crayons on the bedroom wall. He didn't yell at me or hit me or anything. He just said in this real serious voice that the walls weren't a coloring book, and I'd have to wash it off. He even helped me get the sponge and soap and water and stuff to clean it up.

Every parent we have ever met wants his or her child's respect. Nothing drives adults up the wall faster than a disrespectful child. But the converse is also true. Kids want to be treated respectfully, too. In fact, they resent being treated disrespectfully and will go to great lengths to avoid adults who deal with them in this manner.

Our society stresses, at least in words, that everyone has a right to be treated as a person of importance, to be esteemed and shown consideration. As part of this social environment, children also have learned that respect must be mutual if it is to exist at all. Simply put, the more respect we are able to show our children, the more they will respect us. And when we treat them respectfully, we show them positive ways they can act toward others.

The key to achieving this goal is never to speak to our children in ways that we would not tolerate from them—to avoid using humiliation, profanity, sarcasm, shouting, and other verbal violations of our children's integrity. In addition to the quality that this will add to our relationship, it also puts us in a stronger position to correct young people when they are disrespectful. Suppose, for example, that your child curses you. If you can look him or her in the eye and firmly say, "I don't talk to you this way; please don't talk to me this way," then you are on strong ground.

Another way that parents show respect is to ask rather than order, and to express appreciation afterward. We also want to allow children to think and speak for themselves, without putting words into their mouths. Like the father in the opening vignette, we want to treat our children as if they had good sense. We also want to be sure to acknowledge children when they talk to us, and not ignore them because our attention is someplace else. We can be sure to introduce our children when meeting other adults, rather than introducing only the adults. We can wait until later to confront our children about mistakes, and not embarrass them in front of others.

It's easy to fall into showing disrespect for children, because, for generations, respect was considered a one-way street by parents. To become more aware of how our children see our behavior, and to help them know that we do care about respecting them, we can sit down together and talk about the concept of respect. What is it? How do we show it? What's one thing that I could do, or stop doing, that would show you more respect? We can agree to acknowledge signs of respect during the coming week, and to point out times when respect is lacking. Such a conversation might provide a quality parenting experience in its own right, and will almost certainly lead to others.

Expressing Love

> We were all playing Monopoly one night and having a lot of fun. Mom was cutting up—making jokes and stuff—and she got this Community Chest card, and instead of really reading what it said, she said, "If you love your daughter, give her a kiss on the head." And she did.

The love that connects one human being to another is one of the strongest bonds in human life. No wonder love has been such a force throughout history, and is such an important factor in our child's personal history. Yet children do not feel loved just because they are part of a family. They need to see it, hear it, feel it, and thereby experience it through the words and actions of their parents.

We can express love to children verbally and nonverbally, in many ways, and it is important that we develop the ability to do both. Many parents who are able to express love nonverbally find it difficult to say the words "I love you." Sometimes it is easier to begin with a humorous, off-the-cuff approach, as the mother playing Monopoly did. Often expressions of love can be woven into the day-to-day fabric of our time together and we can utilize familiar terms of endearment—honey, sugar, sweetheart, babe, my son, my son—or make up our own—minnow, bug-a-bug, melodious, sweet p.

It's also important to be comfortable with expressing love through touching. Hugs, pats, kisses, strokes, massages, and other physical expressions of affection are essential for building closeness. Parents who are uncomfortable with touching can learn to overcome their inhibitions. By encouraging themselves and taking small steps, they can begin to enjoy such contact. Sometimes professional counseling can help.

Thus far in this section, we have focused on ways of expressing love to our children. If we are married or in some other significant relationship, it's good for our children to see us expressing love to our partners. When an atmosphere of love exists in a home, when children see parents touching and exchanging loving words, they feel more secure. They also learn how to be a loving partner.

A good way to summarize what we've been talking about is to see that encouraging our children, in any way, is a very loving thing to do.

Chapter 5

PLAYING

Playing comes so naturally to us, it may seem strange to think of it as a parenting skill. Yet though we become better at most skills as we get older, the opposite is usually true of playing: children are better at it than their parents. Somehow, as we grow up, we seem to lose the naturalness that makes playing fun.

Yet play provides many benefits for adults as well as for children. Play and its companion, laughter, reduce stress. Playing and humor are good medicine, as Norman Cousins described in his book *Anatomy of an Illness As Perceived by the Patient.* Play helps us re-create our sense of well-being and health amid the more serious aspects of life.

Playing has another major benefit that is related closely to the theme of this book: play is part of the structure on which relationships are built. It speaks in an innate, universal language that lets us connect on a childlike level, bypassing many of our inhibitions and insecurities. "Will you play with me?" is a familiar phrase to most parents. We learned from the experiences of the parents and children we spoke to that this request should not be taken lightly. From roughhousing to board games, from tennis to fooling around with a top hat—the opportunities for play are boundless. Some are as brief as a minute, others last for hours. Play can be spontaneous—a carefree interlude while doing chores—or well planned. Play can refer to any activity that amuses, entertains, diverts us from the usual cares and tasks of everyday life. We will be talking in this chapter about the special kinds of play that occur between parent and child.

We all know people who are so talented at having fun that kids gravitate toward them as if they were Pied Pipers. What's different about them? Do they act in certain ways that foster this positive reaction? By taking a closer look at how such people play, we can learn how to improve the quality of our own play. Later in this book, we will talk more about the content of play, exploring some activities you might choose to play with your children. But first, let's consider some of the attitudes that will help.

Why Many Parents Don't Play

Children use play to explore the world, to develop creativity, and to help them get ready for the adult world. We played "this little piggy went to market"; we had fantasies about being able to fly; we played house; we played school; we played grown-up. All these were joyful games of pretend, devoid of the stresses and anxieties of the "real" world of our parents.

But as we grew up, some of us were taught that play should be put away with the other things of childhood. As a result we end up feeling like the woman who complained about her playful husband:

> I can't help it. It just seems so ridiculous to me for a grown man to be rolling around on the floor grunting and yelling with a three-year-old. But that's what he does every night after dinner

with our son. I just don't think it sets a very good example, and besides, somebody could get hurt.

Where does such a restrained attitude come from? Sometimes, as we grow up, adults tell us:

- You're too old to do that.
- That's kid stuff.
- Act like a big boy.
- Don't be so immature.

Sometimes the puritan ethic comes down on our playful heads with such admonitions as:

- Work is good, play is bad.
- Idle hands are the devil's tool.
- Be serious.
- Don't fool around.

As these attitudes are emphasized more and more, we begin to play less and less. We fear adult disapproval and the embarrassment and humiliation that comes with it. The result is a loss of appreciation for playing. And what we don't value, we don't pursue. Fortunately, we can alter this attitude.

In the first place, we can get back in touch with the child we used to be. That child is still very much alive inside us, and getting reacquainted can be a pleasant process.

Here is an exercise that works for many people: Sit down with a pad and pen for a few minutes and remember what you were like when you were the age of one of your children. Think about how you played then. What did you like to do when you were six? What were your favorite toys, games, and activities? Make a list of some of the ways you used to play. Now figure out when was the last time you did some of these things. Which could you do today or tomorrow? Which might you enjoy doing with your own children? What stops you?

Some people find it helpful to challenge their old beliefs about play not being acceptable by repeating to themselves the following ideas:

- It's fine to play at any age.
- It's okay to behave like a kid occasionally.
- I don't have to work all the time to be a responsible adult.
- Laughing, smiling, and playing are good for me.

Participating

Once we see the importance of playing, we can begin to get involved. This does not mean taking our children to the playground and watching them play with the other kids. Though that can be rewarding, it isn't playing. Playing means participating, joining in the fun. You can push your child on the swing or catch him at the bottom of the slide. Better yet, you can get on the swing yourself and, if you fit, take a turn whizzing down the slide.

Participating is the key not only to playing with our children but to living our own lives fully. Yet we often find ourselves watching from the sidelines instead of being out on the field. We begin to look for comfort rather than adventure and become more and more content just to watch. This is one of those times we can learn from our children: young kids don't like to watch, they like to do. They know that's where the real adventure is.

Perhaps TV is partly to blame for our becoming a nation of spectators. It makes merely watching extremely entertaining and easy. This is one reason we recommend that parents limit and monitor their children's use of TV. True, going to the movies has been popular for a long time, but at least movies involve *going* to the theater, often happily chatting with our companions on the way. Now, with VCRs, we can sit home and have movies brought to us.

It is possible, though, when we do watch TV or a movie at home, to create opportunities to interact and have fun together:

> Watching TV is when my dad and I usually wrestle. Most of the time my mom will be downstairs watching a movie or something that she wants to see and my dad and I end up upstairs looking at baseball or something. We'll just be lying on the bed watching and we'll start wrestling, just kidding around.

Playing is often a contact sport. The touching, tickling, tussling, and hugging that are often a part of playing create psychological as well as physical contact.

Of course, most play activities are certainly not going to include parents, and we do not need to feel guilty when we choose to do other things. How much play is enough? We don't know of any research about the minimum daily requirement, as with vitamins, but we believe that at least twenty minutes each day spent playing with our children, either all together or one-to-one, is a place to begin.

Making the Time

William Wordsworth wrote, "The world is too much with us." He was talking about the intrusions of modern life . . . in nineteenth-century England. What would he think about life in the fast lane of the twentieth century, and how we "lay waste our powers"? In our coming and going, one of the first things to go is often the time we spend playing with our children. After all, we can live without playing, but not without eating, bathing, or sleeping. But playing with our children is important enough to deserve priority in our lives. It's a lot more important—and more fun—than reading every word of the newspaper or cleaning out a closet.

> When I was three or four, my mom would take time out and help me with my dolls. You know, she would play house with me even though she was real busy. And she bought me a small-size tennis racket so I could pretend play with her.

Many parents, especially those who work outside the home, find that picking a regular time of the day—right after dinner, for example—ensures that there will be "room" for play. Once a regular play period has been established, we can find other opportunities to combine play spontaneously with other activities. Taking even a few minutes to play with our children, sometimes individually, sometimes together, will create positive changes in our relationships with them.

Being There

There is a Latin proverb that can be translated: "Do what you are doing." Think about how many times a day we do one thing while thinking about another. If you are playing Ping-Pong with your child but thinking about tomorrow's meeting at the office, you are not "doing what you are doing." And we shouldn't kid ourselves: children know when they have only half a parent playing with them.

When we feel rushed or pulled in too many directions, it's difficult to keep our mind focused on the play. Whenever we catch our mind wandering, we can gently bring it back to what we are doing. Schedule another time for thinking about the office or household chore that needs your attention. By keeping mind and action together, we have the opportunity for getting our heart into the experience. It's all right if sometimes our play must be brief, but while we are playing, we ought to be fully there.

Letting It Out

Children are able to play with spontaneity, freedom, and total absorption. Their imagination and creativity flow easily. All the natural expressions of joy associated with play spring forth without inhibitions—an enthusiastic yell, a hearty laugh, a shout of glee. Not only are they vocal, but their faces and body language accurately reflect all that they are feeling while playing.

Have you ever played with someone whose expression seemed bored or negative? That kind of person is more a wet blanket than a playmate. They dampen our own enthusiasm for the activity. Perhaps they *are* having a good time, but because they keep their feelings inside, we don't know it, and we miss the shared joy of having someone to laugh with.

When we play with our children, it helps if we can act like a child. Acting childlike doesn't mean being irresponsible or out of control, but rather playing with the abandon and freedom of expression that children exhibit. Some parents, because they haven't really played for so long, have trouble letting their feelings show. They feel silly laughing and grinning. Yet these moms and dads can learn to use vocal, facial, and body expressions just as their children do. An added bonus of such self-expression is that the more we look and sound as if we are having a good time, the better time we'll actually have.

Tuning in to Your Child's Delight

People skilled at playing are particularly sensitive to what delights their playmates. Such people know how to make others laugh. They know what excites them and what is likely to spark their enthusiasm. People with these skills are tuned in to their playmates' happiness as much as to their own. In fact, they delight in making sure the other person is having as much fun as they are.

Learn to tune in to your kids, to pick up the cues they're giving about what they enjoy and what they don't. Such awareness of our children's delight will also enhance the joy that we derive from playing with them. By listening for their feelings, we can experience those feelings too. When children share their pain with us, our feelings will be painful. But when children share their pleasure during play, the pleasure is ours, too.

Chapter 6

TEACHING

From the moment we first teach our infant to hold a rattle to the day he or she leaves home, parenting is a teaching art. The skills and values that prepare our children to go out into the world as self-reliant human beings come from many sources: schools, religious institutions, friends, siblings, community affiliations, sports, books, TV, movies, music. . . . But none of what is learned from these sources is more important than what is taught by the child's parents.

The teaching that parents do is ongoing. Every aspect of our family life, from the atmosphere in our homes to the way we greet each other in the morning, teaches the child. Such learning often occurs without either the parent's or the child's awareness.

In this chapter, however, we want to look more closely at how we can very intentionally teach our children specific skills and values. Taking the time to teach our children communicates an unspoken message that says, "I value you. You're success is important to me. I want to help." Peter's description of Saturdays with his dad suggests how important this message is to youngsters:

> My dad and I do something together almost every Saturday. My favorite is building something. He just taught me how to build a doghouse. We had to measure the wood and saw it, then lay it all out so that it would fit together right. Then we nailed the pieces together. I thought it was neat that from all those little pieces of wood we could build a doghouse.

No one has to teach a child to want to learn. A child's curiosity as he or she explores and masters the environment is an inborn gift. Children have a particular hunger for learning useful skills, and we have a tremendous repertoire from which to teach them. From the basic life skills, like toilet training and balancing a checkbook, to hobby skills, such as Peter's woodworking example, to recreational skills, such as swimming or stamp collecting, there is no shortage of material from which to draw.

We don't need a master's degree in education to effectively teach our children, but the few fundamental skills in this chapter may be of help in the sometimes tricky business of teaching our kids without "bossing" them.

Motivation

"You can lead a horse to water, but you can't make him drink." You can, however, make the horse thirsty—in other words, you can motivate him. A parent who attempts to teach a child something the child doesn't want to learn is in for a frustrating experience. To make matters worse, the negative fallout is likely to spill over into other day-to-day activities and into their relationship.

Children are often self-motivated, and that is the best situation for teaching and learning—if we make the time to teach. It's important to do this, even though we're busy. For example, we can make a definite date. Your son wants you to teach him how to ride a bike? Great! How about Saturday morning? Your daughter wants to learn how to use the computer? Terrific! How about starting this evening after dinner? The key is to avoid the typical reply, "Sure, honey, but not right now. I'm busy." Because this response seems more like a put-off than a date for later, it discourages the child and kills motivation.

Young children are very interested in learning to do things for themselves. They are also eager to help out around the house. "Me do it myself," says the energetic three-year-old, though he may be so unskilled that we can do the job quicker ourselves, and with much better results. So we turn our children away by telling them that they are too little, and urging them to "run along and play, dear." Ironically, a few years later, when we do want their help, they would rather run along and play.

With children of any age, it's a mistake to reject self-motivated offers to help. Even young children can be taught simple tasks. They can empty the dryer, sharpen pencils, or set the table.

With older children, it may be a mistake to assume they already know how to perform household chores:

> For weeks we had been going around and around with this dishwasher thing. No matter how I begged or threatened, Jonathan just couldn't seem to remember to put his dirty dishes in the dishwasher. Suddenly it dawned on me to ask him if he knew how the dishes went. He didn't! The few times he had tried had been a real hassle for him. It took me ten minutes to show him, and he's been really good about it ever since.

When motivation doesn't come from within the child, it's up to us to help foster it. To motivate a child to want to learn to do things for himself, these points may help:

- *Be positive about the task.* If we are only halfhearted about the job, children will be even less enthusiastic.

"Steven, I've got a great idea for helping you get your room organized."

- *Emphasize the value of learning to do something yourself.* For example, "Once you learn how to keep your room neat, you'll be able to do it in half the time it takes now. And things won't get lost so easily, like the sweater that was missing for days."

- *Offer your support.* Remember that kids don't always know the best way to do tasks. Especially with young children, it will help to show them how. "Steven, let's mark each of these containers so you'll know where to put things."

- *Let them know how this will help out the whole family.* "It may not seem like a big deal, but it sure makes our whole house look great when everybody knows how to keep their own room neat."

- *Make it fun.* "Let's pretend that we are in charge of a space station. We only have one day to get everything organized before an inspection by Captain Kirk from the United Federation of Starship Commanders."

- *Show confidence.* "You're going to be great at this! Maybe you'll become one of the great room-organizers of all time."

- *Use incentives.* When something they *like* to do follows something they *have* to do, children accomplish the task at hand much more willingly. In the Watson family, room cleanup is scheduled for Friday afternoons from four until five. Promptly at five, two large pizzas are delivered for dinner, to be served only to those children whose cleanup is finished. This sequence of events is different from the use of tangible rewards such as money, toys, or sweets that are more like payoffs to kids to do what we want them to. Children who become dependent on these external motivators may have difficulty developing the self-motivation that comes with valuing the usefulness of the learning and the task. A "what's in it for me" attitude can eventually become self-defeating for kids and irritating to parents.

Timing

Let's face it, we all like to do things when it's convenient for us. Sometimes the need to juggle everyone's schedule and still keep our sanity requires that we take charge of deciding when things will happen. At other times, however, we might try to take our children's schedule into consideration. When teaching a child, it's important to pick a time that will be convenient to both, one that minimizes interruptions so that we can give complete attention. With a little discussion and some give-and-take, it's usually possible to find such a time.

We also want to make sure that we have allotted enough time to complete a lesson. By being sensitive to our child's energy and frustration level as well as to our own, we'll know when to end the session before it gets boring or otherwise unpleasant.

Keeping in mind our children's ability levels is also a matter of timing. Trying to teach a six-year-old how to wash and dry her own hair is going to be unpleasant for both parent and child. Waiting a couple of years until she can easily handle such a task will change the outcome dramatically. To get a better idea of what children are usually capable of at different ages, parents can talk to other parents and their child's teachers, or refer to books on children's developmental stages.

Demonstration

The easiest way to begin learning something new is to watch someone else do it. Whenever practical, try to demonstrate the skill (for example, making a clay bowl). Next, break the skill down into steps (such as kneading the clay), and demonstrate each step before the child tries it.

We want to be sure to avoid saying, "Look how easy it is," for it's rarely easy for someone just learning. Saying so only adds pressure that can become very discouraging when the first mistake is made. It's better to offer a word of encouragement, like, "This isn't as easy as it looks. I've practiced a long time, and I made a lot of mistakes along the way. In fact, I still occasionally do."

Practicing

After we have demonstrated the skill, it's time to let the child do it. Again, if it is a complex skill, it's best to let him or her take it one step at a time. We can coach as the child practices, focusing our comments on what needs to be done in order to succeed ("Okay, now be sure to keep your thumbs firmly on the inside of the bowl"), rather than on what has been done wrong ("No, no. Your thumbs are too loose"). We also want to keep our tone of voice informative and supportive, not critical.

As children practice a new skill or task, they need a lot of encouragement. Breaking skills down into small steps gives the child a sense of accomplishment that encourages him or her to attempt the next step. Our encouraging words are also important during this practice phase, particularly some of the methods presented in Chapter 4: catching 'em being good, showing confidence, and cheerleading.

A good way to practice is to work or play side by side for

a while. For example, you might be making a clay figurine while your child works on the bowl. If you're practicing basketball, you can take turns shooting. Being together during the early stages of learning provides many opportunities for us to give help when it's needed and to cheer our child on.

Acknowledging Efforts

It is important to end the session on a positive note, so that the child is motivated to go at it again later. Acknowledging both the child's efforts and the results can help this happen. For example, "You really worked hard at this. I can see a big difference." Or "I notice you really worked at keeping your thumb steady. The rim of the bowl really shows it."

In order to be able to genuinely acknowledge our children's efforts, it's necessary to have realistic expectations. When we push our kids to learn too fast, the experience is frustrating for everyone. The trick is to develop the patience to let our children progress at their own pace.

Acknowledging efforts requires learning how to accept mistakes. If we display a negative attitude when errors occur—even if the negativity is expressed subtly—our children may become tense from the pressure and make even more mistakes. Instead, we want to communicate the attitude that "a mistake is just another step on the road to success." For example, suppose we are teaching our five-year-old daughter to tie her shoelaces. We have broken the skill down into individual steps and are ready to let her pull the last loop through, making a bow. But instead of a bow, the loop slips out, and she ends up with a knot. At that moment of failure, there is a tendency for children to become discouraged and give up. But a simple, "That's okay; you're getting it. Let's try again" can give her the confidence to persevere.

This does not mean that we want our children to grow up expecting of themselves only halfhearted effort or mediocre work. But the path to excellence is made a lot smoother with signs of encouragement and milestones that mark the steps to excellent results.

Teaching the Teacher

A wonderful way to turn the teaching process around is to let our children teach *us* something. With today's information explosion, by the time they reach the upper elementary grades almost all children know many things that we don't. When we give them the opportunity to show off their learning, they feel proud that they know something that can help someone else. Sometimes, the turnaround comes by necessity:

> We lived in the country and got water from our own well. The pump was rather temperamental and frequently refused to work right. Usually that wasn't a problem because my husband knew just which knobs to turn and push to get it going again. I depended upon him and never learned how to do it myself. As you can guess, one day he was out of town on business when the well quit. While I was tearing my hair out because the plumber couldn't come for two days, my eleven-year-old son said, "Don't worry, Mom, I've watched Dad often enough. I can fix the pump." I really didn't believe he could take care of something so complicated, but I let him try anyway. Not only did he fix it—and you should have seen the enormous grin on his face— but he took great pleasure in teaching me how to do it in case it happened again.

A variation on teaching the teacher is for both parent and child to become partners in learning. This might be a one-time situation, like following a set of instructions as both learn how to assemble a new gas grill, or it might involve

many sessions together in a structured program, such as ka-
rate lessons or attending lectures at a rock-and-mineral club.
These learning activities provide many opportunities for
quality contact between parent and child, and can help
strengthen the relationship as well as individual skills.

Teaching Values

Teaching values is very different from teaching skills. Values need to be taught indirectly. In fact, some people say
values are caught, not taught. In other words, children are
more likely to learn values from what they see and hear in
our homes than from what we specifically tell them.

There are at least four ways that we can help our children
"catch" the values we want them to have. First, and perhaps
most difficult of all, is setting an example for them. If we
want them to value honesty, we must be careful that they do
not hear us telling little white lies. If we want them to respect
the law, it's important that we not exceed the speed limit.
These infractions may seem insignificant to us, but to children, our actions speak much louder than our words.

Second, we can make the time to discuss values with our
children. During such discussions kids can express their
own views and feelings, explore other possible ways of
behaving, and predict the long-term as well as the immediate consequences of different behaviors. When these discussions are kept friendly and open, when we refrain from
pressuring our kids to accept our views "just because we say
so," they will be more inclined to accept family values.

For example, we consider family discussions of television
very important. Let's face it: TV teaches our children values,
and therefore we ought to use it to teach our children *our*
values. We can watch a TV program with our kids and then
discuss our opinions about characters' actions. Other specific

techniques for using television to reinforce our values are presented in Chapters 8 and 9.

A third way to teach values is to play the game "What would you do if . . . ?" "What would you do if you saw a classmate cheating on a test?" "What would you do if a clerk gave you an extra dollar of change?" "What would you do if a friend asked you to look at pictures in a porno magazine?" When everyone in the family takes turns answering these questions, children get a chance to explore some very concrete situations in which their values would be put to the test.

Finally, we can encourage our children to choose values that we approve of by "catching 'em with the value," just as we "caught 'em being good." If we value politeness and they have just thanked a neighbor for returning our cat, we can say, "I noticed how polite you were to Mr. Harding, Jerry. I'm very proud of your good manners." This positive feedback shows them that we've noticed and appreciated their efforts and helps to reinforce the value.

There are times, of course, when children will slip. Occasionally they will choose a value that we don't approve of. The most effective strategy when this happens is to initiate discussion of the situation, rather than just unequivocally stating our disapproval. We can help children evaluate the consequences of their behavior as it affects their own lives. More often than not, if we avoid pressure and criticism, they'll return to the family values. When that happens, its best to avoid saying "I'm glad you finally developed better sense!" Instead, we can praise them for showing the wisdom to rethink their position and invite them to tell us more about how they decided to change their mind.

Chapter 7

MAKING TIME FOR QUALITY PARENTING

"Quality parenting is a great concept," one mother declared. "As soon as my last child is grown and off to college, we're going to have some time for it!"

The all-consuming, never-ending tasks of raising a family—from cleaning, shopping, feeding, driving, and disciplining to managing homework, refereeing fights, and regulating bedtimes—seem to leave little time and energy for quality parenting. Working outside the home or being a single parent makes matters more difficult.

If we could somehow be free from at least some of these daily responsibilities, we'd have more time for quality parenting. Or if we were given an additional four hours every day when each child is born, there would be no problem. But since Mary Poppins isn't going to come and rescue us from our parenting duties, and because a day is still only twenty-four hours long no matter how many children we have, our best bet is to learn how to use our time more efficiently.

There are 1,440 minutes in every day, 10,080 in every week. How we structure our activities within those sixty-second periods will help determine whether we live in a constant state of frustration and anxiety over unfinished tasks and

impending deadlines, or whether we move relatively comfortably through our responsibilities, with time for leisure as
well as for quality parenting.

Most of us are not efficiency experts, and our organiza-
tional skills may leave a lot to be desired. Even if we apply
time-management principles at work, we probably don't
transfer the ideas to our homes. For most of us, there's a lot
of room for improvement and many minutes we can save. By
applying the concept of time management to family living,
we can make more time for quality parenting, and perhaps
even have some energy left for personal activities.

Time management and organization involve skills that
have been well proven in business and industry. In this chapter, we will first present what we believe are the eight most
useful time-saving principles for parents and suggest ways
of applying them to family living. Then we will explore the
important area of building cooperation for family efficiency.
Finally, we will provide some concrete tips for handling
chores more effectively.

TIME-MANAGEMENT PRINCIPLE I:
MAKE AND USE "TO DO" LISTS

It seems like such an ordinary, elementary suggestion, but if
you are not already using "to do" lists, you are in for a wonderful surprise. It is hard to imagine that such a simple idea
can have such powerful results. Not only does making and
using "to do" lists enable us to get more done, but it also
reduces our level of anxiety in the process. Why? Because we
no longer have to rely on our memory to tell us what to do.
Once all our chores are on the list, we can forget about them
for the time being, and focus our attention on the task at
hand. All we have to remember is one thing: look at the list!

You can buy preprinted "to do" lists from an office-supply

store or make your own. Although single sheets of paper will work, we recommend a notebook because it's easier to find and less likely to get lost, and it provides for easy transfer of unfinished tasks to tomorrow's list or for future reference. Lots of little pieces of scratch paper are easily lost and they fail to give the big picture. One master list makes everything more manageable—whether we use only a daily list or also have weekly, monthly, and special-project lists.

TIME-MANAGEMENT PRINCIPLE 2:
ALTER THE FREQUENCY OF PERFORMING ROUTINE TASKS

One way that people in work situations try to manage their time better is to see which tasks can be eliminated. For parents, this usually isn't practical. After all, which of these cherished tasks could we part with: mopping, getting the car greased, cooking, or paying the bills? The answer, alas, is none. Each is an essential part of normal family living.

Rather than asking ourselves which tasks to eliminate, we can look at the frequency with which we do each particular chore and then decide whether it could be done less often without having a negative impact on our family's day-to-day life. For example, if we clean the kitchen once a week (one hour), change the linens once a week (thirty minutes), and dust and vacuum twice a week (an hour each time), we've spent about three and one-half hours. If we could cut the frequency so that we cleaned the kitchen and changed linens every ten to eleven days and dusted and vacuumed every five to six days, we would save about fifty minutes a week. If we could perform these tasks half as often as we now do—that is, clean the kitchen and change linens every two weeks, dust and vacuum once a week—we would cut our time in half, and save over one and one-half hours per week, six hours per month, and seventy-five hours (or almost two five-day work weeks) per year!

Altering the frequency of performing chores, as this illustration shows, can be a subtle yet effective method of making time for life's more satisfying activities. But to do it effectively, we first have to challenge some old habits. Do we really need to do chores as often as we do? Many parents find that their frequency standards are determined either by simple habit, or by their own parents' standards. In either case it will pay to reconsider how often the present situation really requires each chore to be done.

There is an old story about a family recipe for baking ham that mothers passed down to daughters from generation to generation. The recipe ended with the charge: "Always cut off the end of the ham." Finally, one daughter thought to ask her mother why. Her mother didn't have a reason, except that this was how her mother had taught her to bake ham. So the daughter asked her grandmother, who could only refer her to her great-grandmother, who finally gave the answer: "Because that was the only way that I could get the ham into the pan!"

What may have made sense to our own parents or grandparents may not make sense for us. Maybe our house won't be as spick-and-span as our parents' house, but does that really matter? Probably not, and if it means that we have more time for our children, as well as for taking care of ourselves, everyone might come out ahead.

In applying the principle of altering frequencies, the following points are helpful:

- *Challenge beliefs.* Why must we do things the way we've always done them? Might there be a better way?
- *Set new standards.* How often is a particular task absolutely necessary? How often is optimum for our own satisfaction? How often can we comfortably live with (or without) it?

- *Expect some discomfort.* Changing habits isn't easy, especially if we've let them become a part of our self-image.
- *Get information.* Talk to others or read books to get an idea of how realistic your current frequency is.
- *Be flexible.* Try different frequencies until you discover what seems right for your family.

TIME-MANAGEMENT PRINCIPLE 3:
BEWARE OF DIMINISHING RETURNS

The concept of diminishing returns in business is often referred to as the 80/20 principle. Simply stated, it means that 80 percent of the results in most jobs are accomplished with the first 20 percent of the effort.

The extra time we put into household chores may result in only slight improvements. A light dusting that takes only a few minutes might be enough. Would doubling the time result in enough improvement to make it worthwhile? Our homemade spaghetti sauce may be better than a prepared brand, but is there enough difference to justify two more hours of shopping, chopping, cooking, and washing-up? Sometimes the answer is yes. If while cooking we can enjoy ourselves or our children, then it might occasionally be worth the extra time. But if we are taking the long road because of a lot of "shoulds" and other beliefs about the "right way" to do things, we may want to reevaluate.

Suzanne was able to use the 80/20 principle to help change her attitude about the perfectionist standards that she had learned from her mother:

> My mother used to tell me that I should be able to eat off my kitchen floor. Well, I nearly drove myself crazy for years doing it her way. Now, you really can eat off my floor. You'll find a

bean here, a piece of bread there, maybe even some slivers of cheese over there. Nobody—not even me—cares at all and I'm a lot more relaxed than I used to be.

TIME-MANAGEMENT PRINCIPLE 4:
BE WILLING TO TIMESHIFT

With the advent of VCRs people have discovered they are no longer enslaved to the network television schedules but can "time-shift"—record now, watch later. This principle is also applicable to household chores. What law in the universe declares that dishes have to be washed immediately after dinner? If early evening is our low-energy time and we're in an emotional valley, perhaps it would be better if we did something more satisfying to us first, or even postponed the dishes until the following morning.

The key is to know our own physical and emotional patterns. When we are feeling energized and in a good mood, most tasks can be accomplished in half the time they take when we're not at our best. By being aware of our body rhythms and our moods we can shift activities to our advantage.

TIME-MANAGEMENT PRINCIPLE 5:
K.I.S.S. (KEEP IT SHORT AND SIMPLE)

There is almost always a simpler way to do things around the house. Books are filled with time-saving suggestions, from preparing meals quickly and easily to cleaning carpets faster. Appliances like dustbusters and microwave ovens make housework easier. There are businesses that will deliver anything, from groceries and prepared meals to clean laundry, directly to our home.

Keeping it short and simple also means not biting off more

than we can comfortably chew. If we are throwing a party, we don't have to turn our backyard into a Polynesian beach. Such elaborate plans have a way of taking a lot longer to implement than we anticipate. With the K.I.S.S. principle to guide us, we can avoid overdoing things and save the gala productions for truly special occasions, or simply abandon them altogether.

TIME-MANAGEMENT PRINCIPLE 6:
CHUNK IT, DON'T CHUCK IT

Chunking is the art of consolidating similar tasks. Rather than vacuuming one room today, another room tomorrow, and a third on Friday, doing all our vacuuming at once is more efficient. When grocery shopping, we can shop for a week or two at a time. If we run to the grocery store several times a week, much of our time is wasted in transportation or parking, going in, getting the cart, and checking out. Another task worth chunking is cooking. Some people always cook more than they'll serve at a meal and freeze the remainder to be served later. When Marco makes spaghetti sauce for his family, he uses a twenty-quart canning pot into which he puts, among other ingredients, five pounds of sausage, ten pounds of hamburger meat, and assorted cans of tomato products. After dinner, Marco and the kids fill dozens of plastic freezer containers with enough spaghetti and meatballs to feed his hungry boys for weeks. That's a great job of chunking.

TIME-MANAGEMENT PRINCIPLE 7:
MAKE A WRITTEN SCHEDULE

Realistically, none of us are going to follow a schedule 100 percent of the time. However, by scheduling our days and even weeks and months, we can increase the measure of control we have over our time. It's like traveling across country with a map. Once we've planned a route, we're free to take pleasurable detours and side trips without feeling the time crunch that invariably comes when we aren't sure exactly where we are or how we're going to get where we are going. Scheduling brings it all together.

Several schedules are necessary in any family. Each person needs his or her individual schedule, and the family will need a master schedule. There are a number of inexpensive printed schedules from which to choose. Spiral appointment books, three-ring datebooks, and even large calendars work well for different people.

Scheduling is closely related to two other extremely important tasks, goal-setting and priority-setting. When we choose the activities we want to accomplish, we are setting goals for ourselves. Then, when we decide when to do them and put them on the schedule, we are setting priorities. This creates a plan of action which, far from being restrictive, actually gives us a sense of freedom. People who regularly use schedules find that they are taking the time to consciously decide what they really want out of their lives. Their activities no longer control them. By choosing in a structured fashion what to do and when to do it, they get more done and feel better about themselves in the process.

Scheduling quality activities with our children is also a useful way to make sure that such time together stays a priority. The last chapter of this book is designed to help you devise an action plan that includes a schedule for quality parenting.

TIME-MANAGEMENT PRINCIPLE 8:
DELEGATE RESPONSIBILITY

Those of us overly ambitious people who would rather do everything ourselves are wasting a lot of precious time. Since we know best how we like things done, it often seems easier to say, "I'll do it myself." But most effective executives will tell you that this approach not only is inefficient but also can quickly become counterproductive.

Learning to delegate responsibility is essential for efficient use of time. When we can find others to do some of the routine, less-fulfilling tasks, we have more time to spend on our priorities.

The most straightforward way to delegate is to hire someone. Although few of us can afford a full-time housekeeper, chauffeur, and gardener, there may be services that are within reach. The question boils down to one of priorities. Where do I want to spend my money? Most people find it easy to spend money on material things—clothing, cars, electronics, and the like. It's often a little more difficult to spend money on experiences—vacations, dinner at a fine restaurant, a trip, or other intangibles. It's even harder for most of us to spend money on time. How much is an extra hour a day worth to you? What would you pay if we could sell you a twenty-five-hour day? As incredible as it might sound, a twenty-five-hour day is essentially what you are buying when you are freed of your present duties for one hour.

Beyond the objection of cost, many women have additional resistance to hiring help. What stands in their way is an outmoded system of sex-role expectations. In decades past, men went to work and came home to relax. Wives served drinks and dinner, did the laundry, and took care of home and hearth. Although times have changed, many women with full-time jobs still expect to do everything at home themselves. Somehow they see hiring household help as odd or undesirable. One senior executive we know, who manages over three hundred employees, still comes home and does laundry, makes beds, and fixes dinner. She hates it—she'll tell you that up front. But somehow, even though money isn't an issue, the idea of paying someone to do what she could do herself, what "women are supposed to do," is very difficult for her. This might be simply inconvenient or even comical if it weren't for the fact that her children are getting short-changed in the process. There just isn't much time left for them—much less quality time—because their mother is either busy or exhausted.

We all have our standards and values, and some people resist delegating because they really can do a better job themselves. It's true someone else may be able to do the job only 80 percent as well as we could. But is that extra 20 percent worth using up a lot of our time and energy? Consider the 80/20 principle—the time saved that can be invested in ourselves and family may well be worth it. The following is a list of some ways parents are learning to delegate:

- By engaging a housekeeping service to do the heavy cleaning once a week.
- By hiring someone to do the laundry or sending it out.
- By purchasing meals that are prepared and delivered by a local market or caterer.
- By paying neighborhood teens to do simple housework or yard work or to watch the kids while we get essential work done quickly and efficiently.
- By using home shopping services and/or buying through catalogues whenever possible.
- By carpooling with neighbors.
- By sharing a cleaning person or yard worker with a neighbor.
- By exchanging a skill or service we can provide for

housework, meals, yard work, carpentry, car care, or child care. Many communities even have formal bartering clubs.

Cooperation: The Key to Family Efficiency

Efficiency, the fine art of getting the most done with the least effort, is best achieved through cooperation. Anybody who has ever played a team sport has experienced this firsthand. A basketball team in which each individual is doing his or her own thing is quickly outscored by a less talented team playing as a cooperating unit. When the family pulls together as a team, not only are tasks completed much more efficiently, but seemingly unpleasant chores can actually become enjoyable experiences.

> Saturday morning is cleanup time at our house. The five of us tackle the house like one of those maid crews. What makes it fun is that we never work on a job by ourselves. Usually Mom or Dad will be with one of us doing something and the other with the two other kids. We'll sing or tell stories while we work, and sometimes go for hamburgers afterwards.

This cooperative spirit is very different from the conflict and resentment that too often accompany chores. Parents have traditionally delegated chores to their children much as they would to paid employees. That works a lot less well than real cooperation. It also doesn't do much for the parent-child relationship.

The idea was: parents order and kids obey. In reality, even when an order is prefaced by "Would you?" or "Please," children know when there's an implicit demand for performance, and suddenly, like a car engine given too much gas, they stall.

With cooperation, the needs of the situation, not the parent, dictate what is to be done. Children quickly learn what jobs are required for the family to run efficiently. They can be involved in planning the work schedule. Everyone takes part in completing the chores. Parents and children often work side by side.

Since such cooperation is new to many families, some adjustment is often required, as George describes:

> When I was a kid growing up, it was always my job to take out the garbage. I hated it, but I figured some day I'd get married and have kids of my own who would take out the garbage. But then my wife and I took this parenting class at the school where the boys go, and one of the sessions was on winning cooperation. I couldn't believe it! After all these years of lugging garbage, now they tell me that I have to take it out every fourth week like everyone else!

Luckily, George's family functioned so well that he could laugh while telling the story. Cooperation does mean that parents occasionally have to do undesirable chores themselves, but kids are more willing to cooperate when they also have some of the more glamorous or "grown-up" tasks to do.

How tasks are divided is for each family to decide for itself. The key is to involve everyone in the decision-making process. When children are part of the planning, they are much more cooperative in the doing. Of course, the level of involvement should fit the ages of the children: younger kids will be able to handle limited choices; older ones can engage in open-ended discussions.

The following methods have worked for many families.

The List

Do you have any idea how many gallons of water are needed each day to keep your town or city operating smoothly? Could you list fifty responsibilities of the mayor? Could you list the top ten expenditures in this year's budget?

We can't either. But we do know how many gallons of milk our families consume in a week and how many car pools we drive in a month; and, well . . . if we had to, we could estimate the family budget.

Our children, on the other hand, are often as much in the dark about how the family operates as we are about per capita water consumption. They rarely understand how much really goes into the actual day-to-day running of the family. Without this big picture, they can easily see any requests to pitch in as an unfair imposition on their time.

"The List" is an excellent exercise in helping children understand how a family functions and how they can reasonably help out. To begin, call the family together to discuss what jobs need to be done to keep the family running smoothly. List these tasks one by one as they come up on a large sheet of newsprint or posterboard. No job is too large or too small to be listed. Be sure to include the tasks only parents usually do—for example, paying the rent or mortgage, chauffeuring, and cleaning the oven. This helps children to appreciate how much we do on their behalf and it helps reduce the "It's not fair" chant later.

The Rosen family spent two hours one Tuesday night discussing how their family functions. They identified the following tasks that need to be done in their family: planning meals, shopping, cooking, washing up, cleaning the kitchen, making lunches, mopping the floors, dusting, vacuuming, washing windows, scouring sinks, paying bills, driving the car, sorting clothes, doing the laundry, ironing, picking up messes, cleaning bedrooms, making beds, changing linens, watering the plants, emptying the garbage, cutting the lawn, driving the car, cleaning the garage, buying clothes, paying taxes, making doctors' appointments, washing the car, fixing things that break down, making bank deposits, and taking care of the cat. The next night, the Rosens sat down again to review their list. Then they circled in red all the jobs that only Mom or Dad could do, like paying taxes, driving the car, and fixing broken appliances. When that was finished, they asked their children to help decide how the rest of the chores would be divided up so everybody was doing a fair share. When they were finished, they had a schedule of who would do which jobs and when the tasks would be done. They also agreed to meet together once a week to rotate the tasks.

Distributing Chores

This familiar method of distributing chores in classrooms and in the cabins of summer camps can work just as well at home. The first step is to choose tasks from "The List" that will be rotated among family members. Next, cut out a circle about eight inches in diameter from construction paper. Divide the circle into pie slices with a marker, and then label each slice around the outside edge with one or more of the chores. Then make a smaller circle out of a different-colored paper—about six inches in diameter. Put the smaller circle in the middle of the larger circle. Use the marker to continue the lines of the pie from the outside circle to the center of the smaller circle so that they both have the same number of slices. Mark each of the inside slices with the name of a family member. In smaller families, each person's name will appear more than once. Mount the work wheel on a wall or bulletin board by putting a thumb tack through the center of the wheel. Each person checks the wheel daily to see which chores he or she is responsible for. Jobs can be rotated by turning the inside wheel one place each week or month— whatever your family decides.

Another way to distribute chores is to write each one on a slip of paper and then deposit them in a bowl. Each morning every person "goes fishing" and catches two or three chores to be completed before dinner.

One final suggestion for divvying up the chores is to make daily work cards. Using three-by-five-inch file cards, write five chores from "The List" on each card. When the children come home from school they pick a card at random and then choose three of the five chores to complete before dinner. This allows them to avoid their two least-favorite chores on the work card. Having the right to say "no" to certain tasks wins their cooperation for doing all the others.

Tips for Handling Chores

To maintain the spirit of cooperation, we recommend that children *not* be paid for doing regular chores and that the chores *not* be connected to allowances. This is in keeping with a basic philosophy of family cooperation that holds that all members share in both the resources and the work of the family. Wages can be paid for special jobs, under very special circumstances, but we suggest that you emphasize the contribution rather than the money.

Take the time to make sure the children know how to do each chore correctly. Using the teaching process described in Chapter 6, we can guide our kids through each step of the task until it's mastered.

It's important to be both clear and reasonable about standards. One way to do this is to make checklists that break large jobs down into smaller tasks. For example, the checklist for cleaning the kitchen might say "Put the dishes in the dishwasher, scour the sink, wash the drainboards, sweep the floor, take out the garbage, and put a clean plastic bag in the garbage pail." As the child works, he or she checks off each task as it is completed.

In addition to checklists, photographs are handy aids for

setting standards. The McNeils have sets of photographs that show how different parts of the house look when all the chores have been satisfactorily completed. The McNeil children know that they have finished a task when the area of the house they are working on looks as good as it does in the picture.

One of the jobs that can be rotated in families is that of "inspector." As the name implies, this is the person who makes sure things are done satisfactorily. By comparing performance with the checklists and photographs just described, children can perform this duty as well as can parents. It's one of the more glamorous jobs that kids seem to love, and it fosters the type of cooperation we've been talking about.

No discussion of chores would be complete without some tips on how to deal with children who fail to do a job by the agreed-upon time. One possibility is that the person who neglects his or her job must pay a preset fee to the person who eventually does the task. This not only provides a significant consequence to the forgetful party but makes it easy to find someone else to do the job that still needs doing.

The fee could be in paid in minutes instead of money. For example, if Tony vacuums tonight because Samantha simply forgot, Samantha owes Tony double the number of minutes it took for the vacuuming to be done, doing chores that normally would have been Tony's responsibility.

Pete's family found an ingenious way to handle children's "forgetfulness":

> Whenever anybody in the family catches you when you haven't done one of your chores, they can tell you to stop whatever else you are doing and immediately go do it. For every minute you wait before you go start your chore, you have to put a penny in the family kitty. We use the money for movies and pizza and stuff. It makes it fun, but nobody gets caught much anymore.

Clever scheduling can help eliminate the problem of neglected chores. Using what's known as Grandma's Law—meaning "First we work, then we play"—we can sequence events so that chores must be completed before a favorite activity can begin. The activity could be a TV show, making popcorn, or anything else the family enjoys. Remember, these are not bonus activities or bribes but rather regular family activities that are now tied to completing a chore.

Chapter 8

QUALITY TIME AT ANY TIME

We are convinced that it's possible to enjoy quality encounters with children anytime during the day. It's not necessary to wait for special moments, like weekends and holidays, when the ordinary tasks of daily living can be put aside. The purpose of this chapter is to present ideas, or "recipes," for creating quality experiences throughout the day. Whenever possible, we have incorporated the QP factors and the skills of sharing, encouraging, playing, and teaching into the activities. The emphasis is on short, simple "recipes" that require no elaborate preparations. Use them as they are, or let your creativity adapt them to fit your individual style.

Quality Parenting in the Morning

"You've got to be kidding!" replied most of the people we interviewed when we asked them to describe quality moments in their families before school. Morning was generally depicted as a rushed, harried, unpleasant time of day. Kids dawdling; parents ordering, reminding, nagging, and criticizing; frantic searching for lost sneakers and misplaced homework seemed to be standard. The time pressure, especially in families where both parents work outside the home, contributed to making most mornings a hassle.

In any encounter, the nature of the first five minutes determines to a large extent what the rest of the time together will be like. What's the quality of the rest of the morning likely to be when the day begins like this?

> Get your lazy body out of that bed right now before I drag it out!
>
> I can't believe you've got your shirt on backwards again. We've been over this a zillion times.
>
> No, I *don't* know where your sneakers are! You'd lose your head if it wasn't attached."

No wonder few people could recall much quality parenting in the morning! Yet, just as a good breakfast helps fortify our children physically for the day ahead, a few moments of attention, affection, and encouragement early in the morning prepares them to face the new day in a good mood and full of confidence.

We've talked about how important it is to children to enjoy certain events over and over again, until they can count on them happening. While bedtime routines and rituals are common in most families, wake-up traditions can be just as meaningful.

Reveille. It's a military tradition to awaken to the sound of a trumpet. We don't have to be accomplished trumpeters to establish a similar tradition, using a favorite record or audio cassette. In fact, reveille doesn't necessarily have to be a trumpet at all. Sally likes to put on bluegrass music because of the "happy sound and snappy beat. It just makes you want to jump out of bed and start moving." We can play different music every morning or have specific songs for each day of the week. A perfect end to reveille is a hearty good-morning hug and kiss for each child.

Taped greetings. If we're night owls and just can't bear the thought of smiling too early, if our schedule is so tight we can't spare five minutes first thing in the morning, or if we must leave for work before our kids are up and about, we can leave them a taped good-morning greeting. The sound of our voice first thing in the morning can be reassuring. We might even tape a story or song to follow our message.

Reverse snuggles. Kids love to crawl into their parents' bed. Why not reverse this process and crawl into bed with our own sleepy youngsters for a minute or two when they first open their eyes. Enjoying morning cuddling starts everyone's day off right.

Good Morning, America. Taping our own talk show on audio cassettes during breakfast is a great way to have some creative fun. Each person gets to describe a dream he or she had during the night, talk about plans and goals for the day, or make personal predictions about what might happen at school or work (these predictions can be either realistic or fantasized). Older children can pretend to be a talk show host, asking each "guest" to finish such sentences as:

- The best thing that could happen to me today is . . .
- I can help someone today by . . .
- Something I'm afraid might happen today is . . .
- I feel happy when I . . .
- What I hope to accomplish today is . . .
- Something I like about this family is . . .

Save these tapes for replay to see how the goals and predictions came out. They're also great to listen to and discuss while riding in the car together.

Happygrams. Happygrams are brief personal notes expressing appreciation and affection. Kids delight in finding happygrams under their cereal bowl, in their lunch box, or stuck in a shoe. For an added touch use notepaper of different colors and add an occasional sticker. If we make the notepaper available to our children, we might find ourselves surprised with a happygram under our own pillow. You can also put blank notepaper on the breakfast table and ask each person to write a one-sentence happygram for someone in the family.

Morning circle. Some families have the tradition of spending a few minutes together before or after breakfast each day. Parents and children stand close together in a circle or sit around the table, holding hands and giving one another complete attention. In some homes, this is the time for a morning devotional or Bible reading. Other families share a thought for the day, a famous quotation, or a short poem or story. The circle ends with everyone squeezing hands or hugging together. The lovely thing about morning circles is that they stop all the frenetic activity for a few minutes and put the focus on inspirational messages that can give meaning to our lives.

Strong box. The Martin family has an old cracked teapot that they call the Strong Box. Mr. and Mrs. Martin place written notes in the pot with statements designed to help strengthen their children's sense of well-being, such as:

- Today you will find it easy to be creative.
- Today you will be able to concentrate fully.
- Today you will be happy.
- Today you will master a new task.

Sometimes, for the sake of variety, the Martins simply write one word on a piece of paper: *sharp, resourceful, helpful, imaginative, friendly, successful, creative . . .* Occasionally they ask their children what special messages they would like to receive. These, too, are written down and placed in the teapot. Before anyone leaves the Martin house for school or work, he or she picks a note from the strong box and places it in a pocket, backpack, or purse to be read later in the day. In this way the encouraging words from their strong box nourish the family throughout the day.

Fond farewells. The ritualistic peck on the cheek as we say good-bye *is* important. As we've said, rituals give structure and continuity to our lives. In one of Judy Blume's books, the mother and daughter always say the following words when parting: "I love you a hundred million bushels forever and ever, amen." Any family can make up it's own farewell statement.

Quality Parenting Before Dinner

The hour before dinner is crisis time in many families. Working parents droop with fatigue after a day at the office. The pressure from too many tasks to be accomplished in too short a time—cooking, cleaning, laundry, supervising homework—makes many of us feel overwhelmed and irritable. Kids, hungry and low on energy, whine, nag, and bicker with one another. Because they've been separated from us all day, this is the time when our children badger us most for extra attention.

To avoid letting this pressure cause a Mount Vesuvius eruption, we suggest taking a break before initiating any special activities. Now is the ideal time for a fifteen-minute "happy hour" for the entire family. We can serve simple, healthful snacks that won't ruin appetites but will hold off hunger pains until dinner is ready. As we quietly talk or just sit together listening to music, the pressures of the day will begin to ease. Once we've taken time for "happy hour," the following activities can be more fully enjoyed.

TV Critic. TV is used in many homes before dinner to ward off potential crises. Although TV-viewing does keep kids quiet and occupied, few quality interactions occur during these moments. Yet there is a way to increase the quality of TV-watching and teach family values at the same time. Our kids can become "TV critics." In the Mellon family, during dinner, the children are asked to report on what they viewed. The Mellons ask their children questions like:

- What happened on the show?
- Do you think that what you saw happens in real life? Why or why not?
- What feelings did you have while watching? Scared? Happy? Confused?
- Describe each of the characters on the show. Would you like them for friends? Would you behave like that? Why?
- What advertisements did you see? Would you buy the product?
- What do you think the commercials weren't telling you about the product?

The Mellons have constructed a deck of "TV critic cards" for their children. They have written different discussion questions on three-by-five file cards and decorated the back of each card with a drawing, sticker, or cutout of TV characters from the newspaper or from *TV Guide* magazine. Each of their children picks two cards before viewing a show. Knowing the questions ahead of time keeps the Mellon children more intellectually involved and alert as they watch, in order to be prepared for later reporting.

Sharing while preparing. Many kids love to cook. Letting them share in dinner preparations takes a little extra effort from us but it provides opportunities for much quality interaction.

The ages and skill levels of our children will determine the extent to which they can become directly involved in dinner preparations. Children who are able to read recipes and follow directions can be given the responsibility for independently preparing one part of the meal while we prepare another. Younger kids can read recipes aloud to us, gather the needed ingredients, and be guided through the steps of preparing one or more dishes while we explain and demonstrate the process. Preschoolers can be allowed to mimic the cooking processes, such as pouring, mixing, and measuring while we prepare the actual dinner. If we have more than one child, we can involve everyone at once or else focus on one child at a time, while the others watch TV, do homework, or play.

In the beginning, preparing a meal might take longer if we teach our kids to help with the cooking than if we do it all ourselves. However, once they have the necessary skills, we'll save time because they'll be able to take over some of the tasks completely.

Children may enjoy having their own personalized recipe cards and a small metal file box in which to keep them. As they learn to prepare a new dish, they can copy the recipe and place it in their file. Kids love opening the recipe box and seeing how many foods they can prepare. The files are also handy when planning menus, because we'll know what each child can cook independently. This makes it easy for us to know who we can rely upon when we're short of time. Older children can use their recipe files to plan and cook an occasional meal by themselves.

A family affair. We can add quality to the minutes before dinner by giving everyone something specific to do. In addition to the usual tasks of cooking and setting the table, family members can help by performing the following functions:

- *Placemat artist.* The artist decorates plain paper or plastic placemats for the table.
- *Centerpiece arranger.* This person creates a display for the center of the table. It could include flowers, a bowl of fruit and vegetables, ornaments that reflect the season, or a few objects from a favorite family collection.
- *Musician.* Anyone who is taking music lessons can serenade the rest of the family during dinner preparations.
- *Home jester.* Is there one person in your family who loves jokes and who has an endless supply of riddles? Like the musician, the jester entertains during dinner preparations.
- *Storyteller.* A child learning to read can practice reading aloud to the rest of the family with stories from school readers or favorite library books.
- *Food decorator.* As dinner is cooking, the food decorator assembles the serving dishes and prepares the garnishes for each item.
- *Journalist.* The journalist reads aloud articles of interest from the local newspaper and from school newsletters. Short discussions can follow each article as time permits.

To organize for "a family affair," we can let each person pick the job he or she wants each week, or we can write down the different tasks on a piece of paper, place the slips in a hat or fishbowl, and let everyone pick a new job each day.

P.M. Magazine. Families can produce an in-house version of this popular show each night before dinner. One person is designated host and interviews other family members. The focus of the questions is on what actually happened during the day.

- Tell us about something you did well today.
- What was the funniest thing that happened in school or at work?
- What happened during the day to make you happy?
- Describe some mistake you made during the day.
- Did your day turn out as you expected it would? Explain.

If the host has trouble thinking of questions to ask, the family can take time after dinner to come up with questions for future use. These can be written on index cards and kept handy for the next time the program goes "on the air."

Another enjoyable twist is to let family members pretend they are someone else—for example, a movie star or political figure, or even a family pet or favorite stuffed animal.

For an entertaining lesson in good consumerism, the kids can design commercials for items found around the home or for imaginary objects. This will help them become savvy about how commercials are put together, and thus be less impressionable when hard-sell promotions are aired on children's shows.

Accomplishment albums. Since children love to share their accomplishments with their families, we can let them sit at the kitchen table and record their successes in special accomplishment albums while we cook dinner. What's needed to get started is one three-ring loose-leaf notebook, one set each of lined and unlined loose-leaf notepaper, and one package of loose-leaf dividers for each child. It also helps to have a box of stickers, gold or silver stick-on letters, pencils, erasers, and felt-tip markers.

Once the supplies are ready, assembling the album will probably take less than half an hour. Using the dividers, we set up the album to record accomplishments under the following headings:

- *Academic.* In this section specific school skills are listed as they are mastered—for example, "Words I Can Spell" and "Math Problems I Can Do."
- *Musical.* This is the place for kids to list songs that they can sing or pieces they can play.
- *Athletic.* Can your children ride a bike, skate, run a mile? Let them list the teams they are on and provide a rundown of each game and their individual achievements.
- *Social.* Have the kids note when they make new friends, help others, or take an active part in scout troops or other clubs.
- *Personal hygiene.* Learning to get dressed, brush teeth, tie shoes are accomplishments that younger children can record.
- *Helping around the house.* Learning to use the vacuum, cook an omelet, mow the grass are all notable achievements.

While we cook, our kids can make their entries into these albums. Suggest that they not only list their accomplishments but also write a little about how they feel about each success. While the children are happily engaged and we are busy with supper, we can still keep the conversation flowing back and forth, encouraging our kids to express their pride in their achievements and answering with our own pleasure. We can even write a complimentary word or two next to each entry, adding to their motivation to pursue future accomplishments.

Quality Parenting at the Dinner Table

Examples of quality parenting during meals appeared frequently in our research. Although the tradition of mealtime togetherness is still going strong, we all have days when it's nearly impossible to gather the whole family for dinner. Many factors work against us, with busy schedules at the top of the list. Softball practice, guitar lessons, scouts, choir rehearsals, and after-hours business meetings all get in the way. Clogged traffic, a shortage of taxis, and late trains slow the trip home and keep family members apart. The competition from television often means that even when everyone is at home, conversation is scratched in favor of the evening news.

One obvious way to increase dinnertime quality is to simply pull the plug on the TV. There's no way we can really give full attention to one another while the electronic wizard is blaring. The telephone can be silenced by turning on an answering machine, unplugging the jack, or politely telling the caller, "We're at dinner between six and seven so we can't talk right now. We'll call back after seven." Friends and relatives will quickly learn to call at other times. The doorbell will stay quiet if we hang a little note outside that says "We're eating now. Please call again after seven."

Grace before meals. This time-honored ritual deserves to be remembered. Like all rituals, saying grace together creates a feeling of oneness within the family as shared values are expressed. Saying grace reminds everyone of his or her blessings in life and sets a warm, friendly tone for the rest of the meal. It also signals that dinner is about to begin, encouraging everyone to be at the table at the same time.

Most religions have traditional wordings for grace before

meals. Nonreligious families can share a reading, think of their own saying, or perhaps use one of the following:*

> Caring, sharing, being near
> Makes us each feel loved and dear.
>
> This family gives us pleasure.
> Loving and caring is our treasure.
> We rejoice in our good fortune
> And hope others find their portion.

We can say the same words day after day or change them for variety. Many families find that it adds to the feeling of to-getherness if everyone holds hands or touches fingers while grace is said.

Table talk. Dinner-table conversations can be a rich source of family interaction. We recommend focusing table talk on topics of general interest rather than on personal conflicts and family problems. These can interfere with digestion and be damaging to family relationships when discussed at this time. It is better to save tough issues for weekly family meetings and times when there are no distractions.

The most usual type of table talk is the free-flowing jump-in style during which everyone randomly comments on any desired topic. Psychologist Torey Hayden asked several hundred youngsters of all ages what subjects they'd like discussed in their families.† Some of the topics identified by the children that might make for interesting table talk were:

1. *Curiosity questions.* The big "whys" and "how comes" fascinate most children. Why are there people with diff-

---

*Susan Lieberman, *Let's Celebrate* (New York: Perigee Books, 1984).
†Torey L. Hayden, "Conversations Kids Crave," *Families Magazine* (June 1982). Also reported in Tom Licona, *Raising Good Children* (New York: Bantam Books, 1983).

erent skin colors? Why are some people in the world starving? How come airplanes can fly?

2. *The future.* What will it be like when I'm two years older? Five years older? What will the world be like when I'm grown-up? What's it like to have a job?

3. *Current events.* The people, places, and stories in the news interest kids. They sometimes hear bits and pieces of what's happening in the world but miss the larger picture. Dinner time is an appropriate time to fill in the holes.

4. *Personal interests.* Kids like to share what's going on in their lives with their parents and siblings.

5. *Parents.* Behind the mask of "Mom" or "Dad" lies a real person who intrigues youngsters. They want to know about their parents' childhood, schooling, and the early days of their marriage. They also want to know what goes on at work during the day and what their parents do when they are out for an evening.

For an occasional change of pace, we can plan a dinner time discussion around one or two specific topics: friendships, accomplishments, teachers, sports, clothes, computers, local events, and movies, to name a few. Our children will be more interested in the ensuing discussion when they take part in choosing the topics.

"Table talk" is also an appropriate time to discuss moral dilemmas. Karen, the Morrison's twelve-year-old daughter, reads aloud the questions appearing in Ann Lander's column each day. Then Karen, her mother, and her father suggest answers to the questions. Afterward they compare their responses to the advice offered by Ann, and the lively discussion that follows often lasts well past dessert. It's during informal, unpressured discussions like this that our values are best taught to our children.

For table talk to be meaningful, kids need to learn conversation manners along with table manners. Three simple rules will help:

1. Listen with your eyes as well as your ears. Look at the person talking.

2. No interrupting.

3. No put-downs.

Special honors. When we discussed the QP factor "the child is the center of attention," we noted how important it is to a child that the family occasionally focus the spotlight on him or her. Award dinners are good ways to do just that. It's common in our society to honor politicians, sports heroes, officers of organizations, employees who have given years of service, and others deemed worthy of recognition. It seems natural, then, to honor family members when something significant has occurred.

There are many ways to bestow special honors in a family. We can offer a toast with wineglasses filled with grape juice, put a flower in a tiny vase in front of the honoree's plate, provide a paper crown to be worn throughout dinner, and set the table with a special plate or glass for the person being honored. The guest of honor can be encouraged to talk about his or her accomplishment and to express the feelings associated with the success.

The entire family can take responsibility for seeing that special honors are awarded by reporting their own triumphs as well as others'. It's not bragging to tell one's family about the good things that are happening. On the contrary, sharing achievements is a fine way for families to become stronger.

If more than one child deserves special honors at the same

time, drawing straws will decide who gets the spotlight at this meal and who waits until the next one. We don't recommend sharing the honor because its important for a child to be the center of everyone's attention for a short while. Sharing the honor dilutes this effect. Let's not forget, either, that parents should also receive special honors.

Family celebrations. During family celebrations everybody takes part in the festivities. Seasonal and holiday celebrations are obvious times for celebrations, and most libraries offer many books with plans for decorations and menus to make these occasions special. We suggest, where possible, taking the family along on a research expedition one weekend afternoon.

Our religious and ethnic backgrounds offer further opportunities for family celebrations. Some families establish a weekly ritual meal, unique to their family but not tied to any particular tradition. It could be blueberry waffles every Saturday morning, spaghetti every Tuesday night, popcorn and fudge for dessert on Sundays. The choices and possibilities are endless.

Quality Parenting at Bedtime

Enjoyable experiences at bedtime were common among most of the people we interviewed. When compared with mornings or the hour before dinner, bedtime seemed an easier, more relaxed and family-oriented time.

Special activities at the end of the day can help alleviate nighttime hassles. Most kids are less reluctant to turn off the tube or to stop what they are doing if something pleasant is about to happen. Sharing a few relaxing activities with a parent also makes it easier for a child to wind down and fall asleep. When the day ends on a positive note, the psychological closeness that children feel toward their parents will remain with them throughout the night.

Kids are never too old to enjoy bedtime activities. Isabel's children are in their twenties and obviously have no real need for bedtime rituals now. Yet when this geographically scattered family manages to get together, one of the things everyone joyfully anticipates is Mom's lullabies at bedtime— sung exactly as they were when the kids were five instead of twenty-five. Continuing such rituals as our kids get older helps keep our relationship with them close and caring.

Some of the activities that follow will probably sound familiar. Our intention is to expand upon and reinforce some of the traditional ways parents have been putting children to sleep through the years.

Bedtime stories. The bedtime story is one of the most prevalent rituals in this country. A child is never too old to enjoy a good tale. Even when he or she has acquired excellent reading skills, hearing a story is still special. Teachers suggest that we pick books that are slightly more difficult than those our child can read alone in order to expand his or her literary awareness and appreciation. Two excellent aids for choosing stories and making reading an exciting activity are Nancy Larrick's *A Parent's Guide to Children's Reading* (Bantam, 1982) and Jim Trelease's *The Read-Aloud Handbook* (Penguin Books, 1982). Both are available in paperback.

Many families make up stories as a change of pace from reading books. For his two children, Lou made up a series of tales called Buck Bunny stories. Buck Bunny had all kinds of improbable adventures that kept the kids fascinated night after night. Sometimes Buck's adventures had an amazing resemblance to the real-life experiences of the children in this family. Because the stories were made up just for them, the kids felt especially loved. This family's only regret was that the Buck Bunny stories were never written down or tape-recorded so they could be retold to grandchildren.

Lullabies. Singing to children before they fall asleep is another time-honored, bedtime tradition. When we sing the same songs to our children that our parents sang to us, the generations grow closer together. Most libraries have books and even records and tapes that we can use to increase our repertoire of lullabies.

We can sing the lullabies as they were written or incorporate the QP factor "parents make it fun." Alberta starts out each song in a serious mode, then hams it up about midway through. She either disguises her voice, modifies the tune, or changes the words of the song. When her daughter, Judith, laughs and says "Sing it right," she then finishes the lullaby by singing the words "sing it right" to the original tune. "I did exactly what you asked me to," Alberta tells her daughter. "You said to sing it right and so I did." The result is always hilarious laughter and a good time for both.

Another lullaby variation is to take a traditional tune and make up our own words. These words can express our loving feelings for our children, predict positive things that will happen to them, and vocalize our appreciation for who they are and the things they do.

Talk-and-touch time. The few minutes before or after the lights go out are a perfect time for parents and children to enjoy heart-to-heart discussions. It's during these one-to-one times that youngsters often feel most comfortable revealing their innermost thoughts and feelings. Since heart-to-heart discussions go both ways, the sharing skills from Chapter 3 can help us in these talks.

In the Forrester family, Mom, Dad, and five-year-old Brian end their bedtime talks by taking turns finishing the sentence "This was a good day because . . ." We can modify the Forresters' idea by making up our own sentence to complete.

Touching facilitates talking, physically relaxes children, and paves the way for a sound sleep. We can sit close to our child or even lie down on the bed next to her or him. A gentle massage or back rub while talking enhances the feeling of closeness. And of course, a good-night hug and kiss is a ritual that has no substitute.

Ending rituals. After the stories are finished and the lullabies sung, many families have one last ritual that signifies the end of the day. Tucking our child in, kissing his or her cheek, and saying "I love you" is one such ritual. Listen to some children describe other ending rituals in their homes:

> After the lights go out, we pretend we are on rocket ships. Dad shakes our beds and makes this strange humming sound.
>
> Mom winds up the music box by my bed and lies down next to me until the song is over. It plays for a couple of minutes and I always fall asleep during it.
>
> I'm scared of the dark so Mom or Dad takes this can of room deodorant and sprays for monsters under my bed and in the closet just before they go downstairs.

Good-night chants are ending rituals in many families. These chants involve saying certain words over and over. Some chants are short verses parents say to kids or everyone says together, such as:

> Good night, sleep tight,
> Wake up bright in the morning light.

Some chants involve alternating lines between parents and kids. Kent Garland Burtt, in her book *Smart Times* (Harper and Row, 1984), offers the following:

> I love you.
> I love you more.
> I love you most.

I love you honestly.
I love you happily.

Each person adds a different adverb to the words "I love you" until no one can think of any others or until eyes begin to close. Instead of adverbs, we can use quantitative measures, such as:

I love you a cupful.
I love you a pailful.
I love you a boxful.

Or simply use a numeric chant, similar to counting sheep:

I love you one.
I love you two.
I love you three.

Quality Parenting During Travel Time

The daily commute between home, office, and school forces some families to spend a lot of time on the road together—in cars, buses, subways, and trains. These minutes of enforced togetherness offer many possibilities for quality parenting.

Traveling time makes perfect talk time. No one can get up and leave in the middle of the discussion. The doorbell and telephone can't ring and there's no TV to interfere. That's why many working parents of preschoolers prefer to use a child-care center that is near their place of employment rather than near their residence. This extra time traveling together is too valuable to lose.

Kids reading to parents. We hear so much about the value of parents reading to children that it's easy to forget that the reverse is also true. When kids read to parents, it makes the time they have spent learning seem worthwhile and strengthens the youngsters' motivation to learn even more.

Our children can read to us not only from their readers and library books but also from their geography, history, and science texts. This keeps us informed of the content of their classes and opens the door to discussions of the concepts and ideas our children are studying. Finally, our interest in their studies will help motivate them toward increased academic achievement.

Tape time. Traveling offers great opportunities for listening activities. Car tape players and small recorders are so inexpensive that it's possible to listen to tapes no matter what mode of transportation we use.

The choice of tapes is vast. There are educational tapes on a long list of subjects. We can explore different types of music, from bebop to the Beatles to the Boss. If we are traveling by car, we can sing along for added enjoyment. Kids can make their own travel tapes by reading stories, telling jokes, asking riddles, playing musical instruments, or singing favorite songs. We might even listen to tapes made by the family during other times together, such as mealtime conversations and bedtime stories.

Observation activities. Who hasn't played license-plate bingo or alphabet games or, with older children, Botticelli? Enjoying such games together, if the competition is low and the fun cooperative, makes time pass quickly. There are books suggesting games for traveling. Family members can browse through them, jotting down activities that seem particularly appealing. These cards then become handy reminders each time we set out on the road again.

Chapter 9

QUALITY PARENTING
AT SPECIAL TIMES

There are certain times when we are relatively free from the pressures of the clock and many of the routine responsibilities of day-to-day living. It is no wonder, then, that evenings after dinner, weekends, vacations, and holidays were mentioned over and over in our research as the favorite times for quality parenting.

Still, just having the opportunity doesn't automatically result in quality parenting. Instead, in many families, parents spend the weekends shopping, cleaning, or watching a ball game, and the kids are involved in a dozen different activities. We don't have to spend every moment together, but with a little planning, we can share experiences everyone will enjoy.

Special Considerations

Travel guides usually have a section called "Before You Go" that reminds us to get our passports, exchange money, and master key foreign phrases. Preparing for quality activities at special times also requires some forethought about time, money, interests, and skills.

If you feel rushed and pressured, you're not going to enjoy an activity. Make sure that you don't impose time pressure on the family's "free time." Let's imagine that the Martinez family is baking cookies together. They need to have the cookies in the oven by eight because they want to watch a TV special. Carlos is mixing ingredients, but time is running short. Dad keeps saying, "Hurry up or we'll miss the show." As Carlos hurries, he accidentally sends the sugar bowl crashing to the floor. Obviously the fun has gone out of this activity.

Some activities are open-ended and can be stopped at any time. It's best to end these just before the children become bored, while their excitement is still high. Stopping at this strategic point leaves everyone feeling good and wanting more at a later date. It also helps to remember that young children have a shorter attention span than adults. While we might enjoy spending two hours in a museum, a small child may feel that forty-five minutes is an eternity.

If we're trying something different that we're not sure our family will like, it's better to allot a short period of time at first. Listen to how Gregory's family outing turned into a nauseating experience:

> The first time my family went deep-sea fishing in the Gulf of Mexico was terrible. We were on this charter boat for eight hours with a bunch of cousins, aunts, and uncles. Most of us got awful seasick and we felt like we were going to die the whole time.

Because most of us don't have an unlimited supply, money must be considered in planning for special times together. Skiing might be something the whole family enjoys, but if it's July and we live in Kansas, it's going to be enormously expensive to fly to a snow-covered mountain for a week's vacation. That seems obvious but families sometimes get in over their heads financially on vacation and then, especially for the parents, the pleasure goes out of the trip. Even taking the family to a Saturday night movie can take a sizable chunk out of many weekly budgets.

The good news is that we don't have to spend a lot of money on activities. It's a mistake to think that if it costs more, it's worth more. Quality parenting does not have a price tag attached to it. In fact, some of the encounters most treasured by the people we interviewed cost nothing at all. Martha recalls the time all the mothers in the neighborhood woke up their kids at what seemed like the middle of the night to go on a "lion hunt." All the children got out toy rifles and flash-lights and went around the neighborhood hunting for lions. Martha remembers this lion hunt as "one of the most excit-ing things I've ever done."

In addition to considering time and money, it's also impor-tant to try to reflect the interests of each person in the family. There's a thrill and satisfaction in introducing family mem-bers to one's special hobbies. Conversely, everyone benefits from exposure to activities they might never have chosen by themselves.

Keep an open mind—old dogs *can* learn new tricks. Join-ing our kids in activities we've never tried can broaden our own horizons and expose us to new experiences that we might enjoy tremendously. Many of us have learned to ap-preciate rock music or a new sport because of our children's interest.

Compiling a family "interest inventory" will help ensure that everyone's wishes are reflected at various times in the family's activities. To make an inventory, each person sim-ply notes the interests, hobbies, and activities that he or she would like to do with the family on a master list. You can include things that the family already does as well as new ones that have never been tried. The adults will find it help-ful to list experiences they particularly enjoyed as children, though they should be open to the possibility that their children will not necessarily share their enthusiasm.

Another factor to keep in mind when planning special activities is our children's level of skill development. It's no fun for a five-year-old to play miniature golf if it takes ten or twenty putts to get the ball in the hole on a three-stroke course. The child's frustration will make him miserable and dampen everyone's enthusiasm.

Sometimes everyone has fun doing the simple things that young children do—the whole family can work on an elaborate castle in the sand, for example. There are other times when quality parenting means splitting up, so that older kids aren't bored by "baby stuff" and younger kids aren't pressured into taking part in "fun" that's too difficult for them. What is important is that parents and children share leisure time together and that we keep in mind the encouragement and teaching strategies discussed earlier.

Prime-Time TV

If we can't beat 'em, we can at least join 'em. Since many families spend a great deal of time in front of the television on evenings and weekends, we all need to think about how to increase the quality of that activity. We've already talked about how to make TV more valuable to children when they watch it by themselves, but we can also create an atmosphere of awareness and intimacy as we watch together.

We can touch while we watch, sitting close together on the couch, holding hands or with our arms around each other. We can snuggle on cushions on the floor, or cuddle on a bed under a warm quilt on cool evenings. Physical closeness can add psychological closeness to TV-viewing.

Another way to increase the quality of TV time is for the

whole family to help make a master viewing schedule at the beginning of each week. Each person should be able to express his or her feelings about the shows without being criticized or belittled. Then, while the shows are watched during the week, have each person rate them from one, for "disliked very much," to five, for "liked very much." Write the ratings down, and at the next planning session use this family survey to help you make better viewing choices. Another way to rate shows is to have each person complete the sentence "What I liked (or didn't like) about this program was . . ." after a show ends. These responses also can be recorded for future reference.

An in-depth discussion of the content of programs watched will also increase the quality of TV-viewing. We can talk about the characters, their actions, the implications of their behavior, and the values portrayed. Use the talking and listening skills from Chapter 3 to make these discussions profitable. Commercials might also be discussed and evaluated.

Game Time

Board games, playing cards, and puzzles have all been around for a long time. Some families love these games, but many parents told us that playing them was more trouble than pleasure. The chief complaints were about kids bickering with each other, cheating, and whining when it was time to quit. Fortunately, there are some ways to improve the situation.

- *Decrease competition.* Contrary to what many football coaches say, winning is not everything. Winning is not even the reason for playing. We don't have to make a big deal over who wins and who loses, nor dwell on the mistakes that are made. If a momentary lapse costs the game, it isn't a major catastrophe. Instead, empha-size the fun of playing together.

- *Set time limits beforehand.* Children are a lot like locomotives—you have to apply the brakes for a long time before they finally come to a stop. To help come to a smooth instead of a screeching halt, talk about how long you're willing to play before you begin the game. Remember to make the time short enough so that you'll be stopping while it's still fun. With young children, a kitchen timer can be set so that they can be aware of time passing. Also decide in advance what you'll do if the time ends and the game is not over. Will you call it a draw? Will you put the board away care-fully just as it is so that the game can be finished tomorrow? You might decide to set an overflow limit, saying that you'll continue x minutes after the timer rings if the game is almost over. You can also decide not to begin a new game or round after a certain time, so you don't get caught in the middle.

- *Watch your words.* How many times have you heard comments like "You dummy, why'd you do that?" or "That's a stupid move," or "Come on . . . think before you make a play." Sometimes the criticism is more subtle—a groan, a look of surprise, or a shake of the head. If competitiveness gets the best of us, we might even smile or gloat when our opponent has made a poor move because it advances our own status in the game. When we're playing a board game with our children, it's not the time for criticism. In the chapter on encouragement we discussed how we want to "catch 'em being good." When playing together we want to "catch 'em making smart moves" and ignore the others.

- *Teach fairness.* It's almost a basic law of the universe that kids will sometimes cheat at games. Realizing that such behavior is both common and normal in youngsters will help us avoid making federal cases out of such transgressions. If our children cheat, that doesn't mean we're raising moral degenerates; it means that we have an opportunity to teach our children that honesty and fairness are prerequisites for good times.

Going over the rules before beginning a board or card game ensures that everyone knows what's expected. Then, if we do catch a kid cheating, the first time it happens we remind him or her of the rules. Rather than saying, "You forgot the rules" or calling the child a cheater, it's best to simply say, "The rule is . . . and what you're expected to do is . . ."

If we catch the child cheating a second time, we can say, "When you don't play by the rules, it's no fun to play the game. If we're going to continue, you must play by the rules. Otherwise the game is over." Again, avoid put-downs, humiliation, sarcasm, and long lectures. Simply make the point that continued cheating will end the game.

Should a kid be caught cheating a third time, announce in a friendly tone of voice, "I guess you've decided you don't want to play anymore. We'll try again another time." At that point, quietly pack up the game and put it away, ignoring promises not to cheat in the future or tearful pleas to continue. We don't need to administer additional punishment. The ended game and the removal of our attention is enough to teach the child that cheating doesn't pay.

- *End the fighting.* Every game doesn't have to end up a home version of *Family Feud.* Before the game begins, it's helpful to adopt the following rule: We'll speak to each other only in positive ways. This means that put-downs, bickering, annoying gestures, and sarcasm are out. The consequence for breaking this rule is losing one turn. Anyone who accumulates five missed turns is out of the game.

Family Council Meetings

One evening each week or a specific time during the weekend can be set aside for family council meetings. This is the time when everyone comes together to solve problems and to make decisions that affect the family. Building on the skills of sharing and encouraging and incorporating the QP factors of "the whole family does it together," "kids feel grown-up," and "kids can count on it," family council meetings are one of the most powerful vehicles for increasing family harmony that we know. The agenda for typical family council meetings consists of seven items:

1. Complimenting each other as a way of saying thanks for things that have happened during the week.

2. Reading minutes of the last meeting.

3. Discussing old business left unsettled at the end of the last meeting.

4. Distributing allowances and talking about any financial matters that affect the entire family.

5. Dealing with new business that is brought up, such as complaints or problems to be solved.

6. Planning for a special family activity during the coming week.

7. Sharing a treat.

The family council meeting demonstrates that every person is important and that each has a contribution to make. The responsibility for the well-being of the family is shared by all, and the children learn the democratic process firsthand as everyone works to achieve consensus on decisions. As an added bonus, family interactions at other times may be more positive because most problems can be put aside until the council meets. One effective way to do this is to provide a "gripe pot" into which people stuff slips of paper indicating the things that are bothering them. At the next council meeting the gripe pot is emptied and the issues are discussed. By handling problems all at once, we're also using the time-management principle of chunking, and thus saving many minutes that we can use in other ways.

Learning to conduct successful family council meetings takes time and practice. We can gain more insight into this process and sharpen our skills by participating in a parent study group or by reading Dr. Robert Slagle's *A Family Meeting Handbook.* *

Dining Out

A quick look around any restaurant on weekends will attest to the fact that eating out has become a sort of national pastime for the American family. Yet what could be an enjoyable experience is often marred by bickering, complaining, and misbehavior. Still, it is possible to enjoy dining out with our children. In fact, restaurants provide an ideal setting for family interaction because parents aren't busy preparing and serving food and can focus more attention on the children.

Advance planning can eliminate many of the hassles of

*Sebastopol, Calif.: Family Relations Foundation, 1986.

dining out. Choosing a restaurant realistically is the first step. Is the food suitable for your kids' tastes? Is there at least one thing on the menu that each person likes to eat? Will the service be reasonably quick?

Before sitting down, establish guidelines for ordering. What price range is acceptable? May children have appetizers? Drinks? If choosing what to eat causes problems in your family, you may be able to decide in advance what each person will order by taking home menus from restaurants you patronize frequently.

A cardinal rule of going anywhere with young kids is always to bring along things for them to do while waiting. Depending upon the ages of the children, crayons and coloring books, crossword puzzles, a deck of cards, or a joke-and-riddle book can keep them entertained and parents from becoming exasperated.

What if a child doesn't like the food he or she ordered or balks at cleaning the plate? It's probably best not to overemphasize such situations. There's no way to be sure ahead of time how a dish will taste. Mom's lasagna may be a favorite at home, but if Luigi's serves lasagna with layers of spinach between the noodles, a youngster may just turn green. Nor can kids control the size of the portion they receive in a restaurant. Since most adults don't clean their plates when they don't like the food or the portion is too big, it's only reasonable that children be given the same leeway when dining out. Instead of forcing them to eat, it's better to allow kids to learn from their mistakes. Perhaps next time they'll order differently. Of course, we won't give them what we've ordered or let them order something else or the lesson in choosing wisely will be lost.

Accidental spills are no cause for panic or stern lectures. It's better to downplay their importance. Anyone can inadvertently knock over a glass of milk or bowl of soup, and the less fuss we make, the more everyone will enjoy the remainder of the meal.

No section on eating out would be complete without some mention of table manners. To begin with, the best time to teach restaurant manners is at home, not while dining out. An enjoyable way to do this is to spend an hour one weekend "playing restaurant." Set the table, sit down together, and talk about what manners are appropriate in restaurants. Make believe a meal has been served and role-play with your children on different kinds of table manners. Let the children play adult roles while we act like kids. Talk about how manners affect not only our family but other diners as well. Then, should poor table manners occur while dining out, we can deal with the child quickly and quietly. A simple statement like "Jackie, please eat the potatoes with your fork, not with your fingers" is all that should be needed.

It's a good idea to specify, in advance, some consequences if the problem should continue, or if more disruptive misbehavior occurs. The best consequence is immediate removal from the table. One parent might have to wait outside or in the car with the misbehaving child, but the child will probably have to leave a restaurant only once or twice before learning to act appropriately. If you're alone with the children and can't remove just one child, the consequence will have to be delayed somewhat. Simply state that such behavior is not appropriate for a restaurant, and that you will not be taking the child next time the family dines out. Carry through with this consequence next time by leaving the child at home with a baby sitter or family member. The lesson your child will learn is worth any extra expense. However, if the misbehavior is interfering with other diners and the child persists, the entire family may have to leave the restaurant immediately. It's unfortunate, but sometimes everyone has to experience a temporary inconvenience in order for one person to learn an important lesson.

Dining In

Dinners at home can be just as enjoyable and offer as many opportunities for quality experiences as dinners in restaurants. In fact, with a little imagination, families can create some extraordinary meals.

The Rachel family prepares what they call "fabulous feasts" once a month. Each feast features the cooking and culture of a different country. Time in the kitchen is minimized by the use of prepared foreign foods found at the supermarket. If it's a Spanish meal, the radio is tuned to a Latin station or, once in a while, the family makes an investment in a tape—for example, of polkas everyone can dance to when the Kilbasa sausage dinner is over. Younger kids make paper copies of the appropriate national flag for table decorations. Mrs. Rachel collects folk stories and tries to find a short one to tell occasionally. Though everyone participates, the whole thing is treated with a light hand so it doesn't become like a school social studies project.

The Hendersons take a different approach to preparing fabulous feasts. They occasionally plan a meal that focuses on a particular food. Last fall it was apples that had to appear in every dish. They drank apple juice as an appetizer, followed by a Waldorf salad with apples. Next came pork chops smothered with sautéed apple slices, accompanied by a casserole of apples layered with squash. Dessert? Apple pie, of course.

You could also have food all one color, or only food that "crunches."

Once-a-week dress-up nights are another possibility. We can dress elegantly, dress silly, dress as someone else in the family, dress backwards, or dress all in green. Let each member of the family, even the little ones, make one week's decision and, if the instruction isn't taken too literally, lots of hilarity can result.

Marion is a stepparent whose husband's three children come to visit each week. She has taken the girls shopping at used-clothing stores and bought a selection of old, inexpensive gowns to be worn at their monthly formal dinner. No one seems to mind that the gowns are somewhat old-fashioned and twice as large as needed. That only adds to the fun of the evening. Marion's husband and stepson dress in simulated tuxedos by wearing suits, bow ties, and cummerbunds made by pinning pieces of fabric around their waists. As an added touch, everyone has a silk-flower corsage or boutonniere, and on this night the family doesn't just eat, they dine. The table is set with an embroidered cloth, candles, and the best dishes, while soft music plays in the background.

Our religious and ethnic backgrounds also offer opportunities for special mealtime celebrations. Jewish families traditionally set aside Friday evening's dinner as a way to welcome the sabbath. Out come the silver candlesticks, the lace tablecloth, and the best china and silverware. Special foods are prepared and ancient prayers recited. The entire family knows that this night of the week is special and they happily anticipate it.

Holidays and Family Gatherings

Holidays are to the year what desserts are to a meal. They can be a lot of trouble to prepare, but the rewards are great. They are also a wonderful opportunity for quality parenting: "the whole family did it together"; "we could count on it year after year"; "parents make it fun"; and often, amazingly, "everyone is relaxed."

Holidays are so important in families that we don't have to confine ourselves to the usual, traditional days. We should celebrate them, of course, but we can also create and celebrate as many holidays as we wish. In our interviews we found that some families celebrate:

- the first day of each season
- the full moon
- the first or last day of the school year
- a pet's birthday
- the anniversary of moving into the present home
- "unbirthdays"
- someone else's birthday—a living, historical, or fictional person the family admires
- "no reason" holidays—a date is picked from a hat on the first day of each month to determine when the "no reason" celebration will take place
- trivia day—when some invention or historical event occurred that's of interest to the family.

Letting our imaginations run wild while creating new holidays can itself be fun. Holiday ideas can come from such sources as our own childhood, celebrations that friends and relatives enjoy, or reference books on holidays.*

In many families, the major national and religious holidays are the times when the extended family congregates. Grandparents, parents, siblings, aunts, uncles, and cousins all come together to renew old ties and strengthen new ones. Because the crowds, confusion, and changes in daily routines sometimes can turn the celebration into a time of conflict, it's useful to take certain precautions.

Children fare best when they maintain their usual schedules as much as possible. Late meals generally mean

*Two books we particularly recommend are Susan Lieberman's *Creating New Family Traditions* (New York: Putnam, 1984) and Gloria Gaither and Shirley Dobson's *Let's Make a Memory* (Waco, Texas: Word Books, 1978). The latter has a strong Christian orientation and focuses on religious as well as secular holidays.

cranky kids. So does a lack of sleep. Whenever schedules must go completely out the window, it will help to rely on snacks and naps.

The moment when all the family is gathered around the table watching the turkey being carved is not the time to criticize our children's table manners or attempt to coerce them into trying new foods. As we advised in "Dining Out," we want to save the teaching moments for the privacy of our home.

When our children need to be disciplined, the best method is to remove them to a time-out area, as far away from relatives and other distractions as possible. Nagging, threatening, bribing, and spanking, not very effective tools for disciplining youngsters under any circumstances, work even less well in front of relatives.

Since it's all too easy for squabbling kids to get their parents squabbling with each other, it's best not to get embroiled in kids' fights. An objective adult, preferably one without kids, or at least one whose children are not involved in the fight, can mediate and help the kids find their own solutions. Sometimes difficulties arise because the adults compare one cousin with another, thereby fostering competition and jealousy between the kids.

To foster close relationships between the generations, try seating kids between the adults at the table rather than clustered by themselves at one end. Make sure to include the children in the mealtime conversation. (See the suggestions for table-time topics of conversation in Chapter 8.) It's a broadening opportunity for youngsters to hear their relatives' views on subjects that have been discussed within the children's own family.

Another good idea is to plan some activities the whole extended family can enjoy. The Longo family plays Michigan rummy after holiday dinners. The kids count on this year after year and look forward to the lively card game. Another family has songs they always sing together. They have even compiled the favorites into a short songbook. Everyone has a copy so the whole family can join in without having to remember all the words. A touch football game seems to be a mandatory activity at the Simpsons' family gatherings.

Collecting living legends, unique stories that are passed down from parents to children, can be fun for everyone in the family, especially if many generations are gathered together. Parents, grandparents, or other older relatives might describe the family's arrival in America. Other adults might tell of unusual and memorable moments someone in the family experienced or notorious parental escapades from their youth. Some families tape or write down these stories. You can make your own record or use the blank books with decorative hard covers that bookstores sell. Add old photographs that are appropriate to the tale, or have members of the family draw illustrations.

We can preserve the memory of holiday gatherings by dividing different recording tasks among the family. Someone becomes the family photographer, taking snapshots throughout the day. Another is the family reporter, writing down brief synopses of all the interesting events and conversations that occur. Yet another compiles family recipes, while someone else creates a family tree. Larger families can rotate the jobs or have more than one person involved in each of these activities.

Because of geographical distances, many families can't gather together as often as they would like. Yet, as we noted in Chapter 2, it's important for children to feel connected to their relatives. The Moores, who live in Ohio, have devised an ingenious way for keeping in touch with family on the West Coast. Once or twice a month, on weekends, the parents and children gather for an hour of letter-writing.

To make corresponding an enjoyable family activity, the

Moores have assembled a writing supply box. In this box is assorted stationery, lined paper, construction paper, personalized notepads, picture postcards, pencils, colored felt-tip pens, crayons, stickers, stencils, assorted rubber stamps, gummed alphabet letters, and glitter.

The Moores make it easy to know what to write about. They have cut down the sides of two supermarket cartons and labeled one "Family News Box" and the other "Local News Box." They fill the Family News Box with samples of schoolwork and artwork, short notes about individual achievements and milestones passed, menus and placemats from restaurants where they have dined, souvenirs from outings and trips, news about the family pets, short summaries of family activities, favorite jokes and stories, recent family photographs and favorite recipes. They fill the Local News Box with interesting articles from the daily paper, postcards showing local landmarks, brochures from the chamber of commerce about local attractions, and photographs or drawings of the area.

With these boxes as a resource, writing to relatives becomes easy. The Moores first write individual letters. Each person chooses a piece of writing paper and an item or two from the news boxes to write a few sentences about. Sometimes they just send the letter; other times they clip or staple the letter to the news item and mail both.

A spin-off of the Moores' method of keeping in touch with relatives is the round-robin letter. The entire family uses the same sheet of paper, each person adding a paragraph or two to the letter. Graffiti letters are similar. Using a large sheet of writing paper with a heading such as "My Favorite Foods," "Movies I Like," "Places I Want to See," or "My Wish List," everyone writes as many responses as he or she likes for the particular heading.

In addition to writing letters, we can design homemade special-occasion cards. Relatives will love receiving birthday wishes, holiday greetings, or thank-you notes made and signed by the entire family.

Family Outings

Every city or town offers some possibility for a family outing. It could be a park, a zoo, a museum, a lake, a fair, or a trip to Uncle Joe's. Using the suggestions at the beginning of this chapter regarding money, time, interest, and skill level can help us choose where to go.

To make any family outing more pleasant and meaningful, it pays to involve the kids in the planning before leaving home. Perhaps the best time to make these plans is at the weekly council meeting. Everyone is already together and the spirit of cooperation is in the air. Planning outings at the end of the council has the added benefit of ending the meeting on a high note after the seriousness of solving problems. In addition to planning where you'll go, be sure to cover approximately how long you'll stay and what you'll do about eating.

On the day of the outing, it's important to go over ground rules for the excursion. You'll also need to decide whether everyone will stay together the entire time or occasionally separate. Most older kids will want to "do their thing" for a while and then come back together to share experiences. Finally, if you do decide to separate, be crystal clear about meeting times and places. Writing these down and synchronizing watches are precautions that can save much frustration later.

You'll also want to make it clear how much, if any, souvenir-buying the children will be allowed, and whether it's your money or theirs that will be used. Either way will work, as long as the expectations and limits are understood ahead of time. And, as any parent who has been through the experience will attest, it's much easier to make these decisions at home than to confront a whining kid at the souvenir stand while the world looks on.

Food is another area where some planning can short-circuit a bad time. Since kids never seem to leave their appetites at home, taking some pocket munchies along will help. Trail mixes—tasty combinations of nuts and dried fruit—are excellent for this purpose. It also helps to let everyone know ahead of time when meals will be eaten. This tends to silence the constant "When are we going to eat?" lament that can try everyone's patience.

Sooner or later, most family outings include a day or two at an attraction like Disney World or a local amusement park. Whether big or small, world-famous or local, these places can be monsters. They seem designed to wear us out before we wear them out. In other words, the first rule is: don't stay too long. Though the hours may be from eight in the morning until midnight, the fun is almost guaranteed to run out before the clock does. Be reasonable in estimating the amount of time that your family can handle "having fun." You can avoid the hasslcs of "just five minutes more" or "just one last ride" by setting time limits beforehand. Sometimes it's possible to siesta in a hotel room during the late afternoon and then return to the attraction in the evening.

Another snake lurking in most attractions is the twisting line. You may have to wait an hour for a ride that lasts less than a minute. To make the wait tolerable, not terrible, take along a lightweight drawstring bag with such things as paperback story books, puzzle books, magnetic games, crayons, and small clipboards. Try playing alphabet and other word games while waiting, or some of the games you play in the car. Walkmans are great, and you might even want to invest in lightweight folding camp stools if you're planning a trip to a popular attraction where long lines are inevitable.

It also pays to keep in mind that meteorology is an imperfect science. The best way to cope with bad weather is to have an alternative in mind. Since many of these outdoor places can't be visited on bad days, it helps to research the museums, movies, and malls in the area.

Finally, try to avoid getting hooked by minor complaints. Everyone gets tired, bored, or irritated at times on any vacation. It's usually best to respond to our kids' complaints with just a nod of the head and a simple "I understand." Continued complaints can be completely ignored. The less we respond, the quicker the complaining will stop. On the other hand, sometimes real problems do arise. If your youngster's gripe is legitimate, listen, respond, and try to come up with a solution together.

Vacations

Some families camp out in the woods, some visit relatives, go to hotels and resorts, tour America, cruise on boats, stay at dude ranches, travel abroad, or rent vacation homes. We've even known families who had marvelous vacations exploring their own cities and never leaving home overnight.*

To make any vacation a quality experience, try to involve the kids in the planning. They need to know where they're going, why, and what to expect. Take the time to read guidebooks together, study maps, and learn as much as possible ahead of time about the trip. This planning also is an opportunity to clarify expectations: if the kids think they'll be eating all their meals at McDonald's but you're planning to sample restaurants that feature local specialties, there's going to be a conflict. It's much easier to handle disagree-

*Linda Albert and Elaine Shimberg, *Coping with Kids and Vacation* (New York: Ballantine Books, 1986), 96–104.

ments and disappointments before leaving home than after arriving at the destination.

It is also important to be realistic in your expectations. Even vacations with an educational focus should be fun. Overscheduling can leave everyone exhausted at the end of the trip, and feeling in need of a vacation after the vacation. Always include plenty of unscheduled time in your plans.

"Something for everyone" is a good policy for a family vacation. We don't have to please all the people all the time, but we can please all the people *some* of the time!

It helps to keep daily routines like meals and bedtime as close to normal as possible, even on vacation.

Finally, no vacation has a chance to succeed unless we remember to pack our sense of humor. Since plans, however well made, never turn out perfectly, it's just as well not to become slaves to our plans. If we become discouraged when things don't go well, our children will pick up on the tension. It's much better to accept, adapt, and learn to laugh at the unexpected inconveniences that inevitably occur.

Making Memories

Shared memories are like strands of yarn that connect the past to the present and knit families close together. Recalling past events gives families a sense of a unique shared history. Such memories also allow a family to relive the feelings of closeness and fun they have had together.

Collecting these memories, as well as recording present events, can provide hours of enjoyment. Some creative possibilities for collecting and storing memories are:

- *Photograph albums.* You can make the albums more meaningful by adding one or two lines of explanation—or fun—below each picture.

- *Family scrapbooks.* In addition to photographs, scrapbooks can contain newspaper articles, restaurant placemats, airline ticket receipts, postcards, maps—any items that are associated with a particular experience. Short descriptions can be written by individual family members or as a group project.
- *Treasure boxes.* Collections of memorabilia from outings and trips are assembled and stored together in clearly labeled shoe boxes or small cartons. These boxes accommodate bulky items that can't be pasted into scrapbooks.
- *Logbooks.* Use them to record short accounts of the highlights of each day or week. You can make it a family ritual to take out the logbook at a certain time each week or month to add entries.
- *Patchwork wall hangings.* If your family travels together often, buy a souvenir patch at each place you visit. Then sew the patches onto a large square of fabric or a plain felt banner to be hung on the wall.
- *Collages.* On a large piece of newsprint or posterboard, paste memorabilia from a trip or outing. Add appropriate words cut from newspapers and magazines, stickers, glitter, crayon drawings, and any other decorative materials you wish. Frame and hang the collage, or tack it to a bulletin board.

Recording family memories is only half the fun. The rest of the fun comes when we sit down together and browse through the albums, logbooks, treasure boxes, and other keepsakes, playing "remember when" and savoring these memories of special times with our families.

Chapter 10

QUALITY PARENTING IN NONTRADITIONAL FAMILIES

Across the country, the "traditional" family—Mom, Dad, and kids living under one roof—is now in the minority. The "nontraditional" homes—the single parent or the blended family—make up the majority. If present trends continue, it's likely that some time during the 1990s nontraditional families will be considered the norm throughout America.

Words like "broken home," "motherless," "fatherless," or "stepchild" used to be said pejoratively, but now there is a growing acceptance in our society of the changing American family. The media at one time portrayed children from nontraditional homes as having more emotional, behavioral, and learning problems than other children. Today's prime-time shows feature a wide variety of family configurations, and almost always in a positive light.

The negative image of the nontraditional family resulted in large measure from confusing the structure of the family with the dynamics of family life. The truth is that any family structure can be effective for raising kids to be well-adjusted, cooperative, respectful, and successful. We all know nontraditional families that work well, and traditional nuclear families that don't. It's the quality of life going on inside the structure that counts. What is the home environment like? What kind of interactions take place among family members? What perceptions do people have of themselves and of each other?

In this chapter we'll explore ways quality parenting concepts can be applied to the specific problems and opportunities of nontraditional families.

Single-Parent Families

Loss is the common denominator in most single-parent families. While coping with the loss of a spouse, the adult must learn to juggle career, children, and daily living tasks alone. Even when the loss is due to divorce and may be tinged with a sense of relief, the single parent must face the end of a dream.

Children in single-parent families must adjust to living with only one biological parent in the home. Sometimes, they may also have to cope with a change of residence, school, and even friends during the transition from two-parent to single-parent living.

To make matters even more difficult, single parenting often becomes budget parenting because the income that once sustained one household must now support two. A tighter budget may mean giving up favorite activities like summer camps, special lessons, and Saturday-night pizza.

Handling Loss

Loss is always accompanied by a tremendous amount of emotion: grief, pain, anger, resentment, guilt, and sadness. Most psychologists agree that the best way to deal with these feelings is to allow them to surface and be expressed verbally rather than to try to hide them and make believe everything's fine. Here's how Elaine's mother helped her daughter handle her feelings after the divorce:

> One Saturday morning about a week after the divorce had become final I had come into the den, and Elaine (age eight) was sitting in the big armchair—the one her father used to sit in—watching cartoons. She had the quilt around her and looked real cozy, but I could tell from the expression on her face that something was wrong. When I asked what was bothering her, she acted as if she didn't even hear the question. I waited for a commercial, then knelt down beside her and put my hand on her arm and said, "You look real sad, honey. Do you miss Daddy?" Her eyes filled up with tears, and she just nodded. I told her I knew how tough it must be for her and that it was pretty tough for me, too. She asked me why her father couldn't come back, and I told her again that the two of us had decided that we just couldn't live together anymore. She whispered that it wasn't fair, and eventually she told me how angry she was, and mostly at me. Somehow, she had decided I should have done more to keep Steven happy, and if I had, we'd still all be together. I let her get it all out. I didn't get defensive or tell her that it wasn't all my fault, because I figured that right now she just needed to get it out.

Elaine's mother did a good job in encouraging and enabling Elaine to feel safe about sharing her feelings. This will actually strengthen their relationship as it helps to heal Elaine's pain. Her mother might also want to tell Elaine some of her own feelings of guilt and sadness, so long as she doesn't go overboard and treat Elaine more like a confidante than a daughter.

In addition to listening and responding to help our children deal with loss, it's also important to express confidence in their ability to handle a difficult situation. We want to assure them that they will eventually pull through and be okay. We can acknowledge the negative feelings, and that dealing with loss and change is not easy, but we need also to add encouraging words like, "You're right, it's not a happy time for you right now, but I know you have what it takes to pull through." And, of course, we always remind them, "I'm here when you need me—let's talk again."

A common pitfall in situations of loss is the tendency to overprotect or pamper kids and thereby frustrate their need for independence. When we see our children sad and in pain, and especially when we think we're to blame, it's easy to want to "make it up to them." Sure, they'll let us make their beds, pick up their clothes, and do things they could very well do for themselves, but they'll become dependent and spoiled in the process. Even worse, they might expect teachers and other adults to give them these same special services. Our children may even learn that to get such special services from adults, all they have to do is look a little sad and pitiful. So rather than overprotecting or pampering our children to help them deal with loss, it's best to let them do things for themselves and to provide support through our quality-parenting skills.

Winning Cooperation

Most parents face a time crunch, but single parents face the biggest crunch of all. Any of us who work all day and manage a home and family by ourselves during "off" hours have certainly found that there are too few hours in each day. The time-management principles in Chapter 7 can be lifesavers for single parents.

Without a spouse's help, we'll probably have to ease up on routine tasks. Our homes may get a little dustier between cleanings, and our floors may look a little duller, but those things are much less important than quality time in the family—as one little girl attests:

> We were all doing our chores one Saturday, and the sink was full of dirty dishes, but my mom said, "Come on. It's too pretty a day to do dishes—we're going to the beach!" She said that forty years from now I wouldn't remember having done the dishes, but I would remember going to the beach.

It also pays to apply the K.I.S.S. principle. The less time we have, the more we want to "keep it short and simple" by finding easier ways of doing things and not taking on extra responsibilities.

Delegating responsibility and engaging paid household help would be a godsend to any single parent, but this may not be feasible when managing a family on one income. So sharing the household tasks with children often becomes the only means of lightening the parent's load. Surprisingly, this may be a blessing in disguise, for most kids are willing to pitch in when they see the real need. The suggestions for distributing chores discussed in Chapter 7 are just as applicable in single-parent families as in traditional ones and will work as long as the parent is on guard against the natural tendency to overprotect children that we spoke of earlier. It's much better to stimulate their independence and let them perform the household tasks that are appropriate to their age and skill level than to do everything ourselves.

Breaking with the Past

Many single parents make the mistake of living in the past and trying to keep everything the way it was. They believe that for the sake of continuity it's important to make as few changes as possible. In reality, balance is called for. On the one hand, it is useful to emphasize the restructuring that has occurred, and to acknowledge the fact that this is now a new and different family. On the other hand, we do want the continuity that says to our children that our roots are solid and our sense of family is strong.

One way to handle these two conflicting needs is to discontinue some of the family's rituals and traditions, and to maintain others. Although discontinuing some of the rituals goes against the QP factor "we could count on it," it does emphasize that some things will have to be different. Acknowledging this helps children put aside the common fantasy that maybe someday, somehow, their parents will get back together and everything will be just the way it was.

In choosing which things to discard and which to continue, think about whether the former spouse is essential to the activity. For example, if popping corn and snuggling together during a favorite Thursday-night TV show is a favorite tradition, there's no reason this can't continue. We may want to handle other matters the way Fern did:

> One of the things that the kids really missed at first was our summer camping trip. But there was just no way that I was going to trek out into the national forest with three kids, a dog, and an old station wagon. Besides camping was Ted's thing. I never really liked it that much anyway. The kids and I talked about it for a long time, and they almost had me convinced to try it, but sanity prevailed and now we go to a small resort on a lake instead. They still go camping with their father.

This mother was able to help her kids deal with the reality of their new life by beginning a new tradition and acknowledging that some of their good experiences and memories would involve their father, not her.

Establishing their own traditions helps single-parents rebuild a sense of family. The more new rituals and routines we incorporate into our daily lives, the more our sense of identity as a new family will be established.

In a single-parent family, the "we" in the QP factor "we did it all together" means one parent and the children, not both biological parents making believe that all is well and not much has changed. We've seen many families who, especially on holidays, celebrate and do things together in an attempt to make the family seem "whole" to the kids. This is usually a mistake, for it confuses the children as to where one of their families ends and the other begins. It gives them false hope that their parents might reunite someday. The only time it's really appropriate for the original family to be together is when there really is no choice for celebrating separately, such as at weddings and graduations.

Blended Families

While "blended family" is often used as a synonym for "step-family," in reality the term describes families where two adults raise the children in situations like the foster family, adoptive family, grandparent family, as well as the step-family. The stepfamily, though, is by far the most common. About one American child out of five now lives in a blended family and the numbers show no signs of decreasing. Because both a mother figure and a father figure live in the same home with the child, many people mistakenly believe that blended families can function just like traditional biological families. This simply isn't the case.

To begin with, most members of blended families have experienced significant losses. There may be a biological parent elsewhere who affects everyone's life. Even if that parent is deceased, his or her memory must be dealt with. In addition, family members come to the blended family with different backgrounds, experiences, and ways of doing things.

Coping with Crises

It's not at all unusual for blended families to find themselves in trouble. When it becomes apparent that everyone isn't going to form instant, loving relationships, when the power struggles and loyalty conflicts surface, and when the adjustment difficulties seem endless, a full-blown crisis can erupt. Fortunately, such problems also present opportunities. In fact, the Chinese word for "crisis" also means "challenge" or "opportunity."

A crisis gives us a chance to deal openly with the negative feelings that led up to it, as well as those created by the crisis itself. Sometimes, though, we ourselves are so distraught that we aren't able to hear our children's problems in the family. When this happens, finding a sympathetic ear for ourselves can bring great relief. A trusted friend, a member of the clergy, or a professional counselor can fill this role. Once we're dealing effectively with our own emotions, we can better help our children deal with theirs.

Any prolonged crisis causes a very gloomy atmosphere in the home. The problems can seem insurmountable and the negative feelings can reduce our strength and stamina to cope. One way to break this cycle is through some plain old fun. Simple though it sounds, a little laughter can help make everyone feel better and begin to see the brighter side of things:

> We started having game time every evening after dinner. Chutes and Ladders was the big favorite, but it wasn't the game so much as the cutting-up that went with it. It really gave us a chance to let off some of the steam that had been building up around here.

Of course, playing games and cutting-up together is not going to solve whatever major issues are facing this family.

They can't ignore the problems that brought about the crisis in the first place. Talking together, problem-solving, and even seeking professional help are all steps they might want to take. Playing and having good times together won't negate the difficulties. They will make them more bearable until solutions can be found, and perhaps even prevent the crisis from turning into a catastrophe.

Compiling a family interest inventory (page 119) will help everyone to realize that, despite the present crises, good times are a part of this family's life. Actually scheduling when activities and outings will occur will give family members something positive to anticipate.

It may seem awkward and even phony to play and have fun when serious problems are hanging over our heads. That's because we're not used to the juxtaposition of crisis and pleasure. Yet, if we stick with it, the discomfort will lessen and perhaps even disappear entirely.

When coping with a crisis, it helps to set aside specific times to deal with the problems. The weekly family council meeting is a good place to start, but if once a week isn't enough, problem-solving times can be scheduled at a specific hour every day or two.

The Bergmans, a foster family with five children, got tired of the endless hassles that came up all evening long. They found themselves feeling very negative about the kids, and even with each other, because there never seemed to be any time when they weren't dealing with problems. So they decided to have a "minimeeting" each day just after dinner. At this time they deal with the minor skirmishes that come up each day, saving the major problems for the longer council meeting. Handling problems at this minimeeting leaves the Bergmans free to enjoy the rest of the evening.

Building New Relationships

It is a major task for an adult to build an effective relationship with a child he or she is living with but has not parented since birth. First, the adult must choose whether to be friend, confidant, parent figure, mentor, or role model* and the choice depends upon the needs of everyone involved. For example, a twelve-year-old who lives half the time in a stepfamily and half the time with his mother might fare much better with his stepmother as a close friend and confidante, rather than as another parent. And in any blended family relationship, the adult may need to shift back and forth between roles as circumstances dictate.

Forming a close parent-child relationship in a stepfamily involves almost the same steps as forming a friendship with another adult. When we meet another person we would like to become close to, we spend time together, talk together, do things together, have fun together. But getting to know each other also means getting to know each other's dreams, wishes, fears, and preferences. The skills for sharing can help our children get to know us better, as we reveal details of our lives to them, and also encourage them to share with us more about who they really are.

The time spent playing with our stepchildren or teaching them how to do things is time spent building a bridge between them and us. When the relationship is new, such a bridge is very weak and can be easily blown apart by the high winds of crisis. As we have more positive experiences together, the bridge becomes gradually reinforced, until it is like a steel suspension bridge capable of withstanding many storms.

The encouraging skills are particularly helpful in building

*Elizabeth Einstein and Linda Albert, *Strengthening Your Stepfamily* (Minneapolis: AGS, 1986), 58–59.

relationships with children, for children grow emotionally close to those who cheer them on. But sometimes, when stepchildren or foster children begin to feel close to the "new" parent, they feel disloyal to the biological parent of the same sex. To protect themselves from this loyalty conflict, they sometimes create psychological distance by misbehaving. If this happens often, we can end up feeling that we've inherited a real troublemaker. This is where the encouragement technique of "catch 'em being good" can be especially important. By noticing and commenting on positive behavior we can keep our perspective clear until the conflict subsides.

Showing affection is also important, though, if the child is used to a very reserved style with little touching or hugging, a new stepparent who enjoys huge bear-hugs may make the child very uncomfortable and actually slow the growth of the budding relationship. If we see that physical displays of affection are not well-received, it's best to move slowly, taking our cues from the child. On the other hand, reserved adults will need to make an effort to be more demonstrative with "cuddly" children. Otherwise the child may interpret reserve as a sign of rejection.

Establishing a New Identity

Blended families often don't feel like "real" families. The lack of a common history and shared memories weakens the family's sense of identity. To remedy this situation, we need to carefully plan experiences that everyone enjoys and that will begin to define the uniqueness of the new family.

When we remember times we've shared together, we generally think of quality time. All the activities we have previously suggested will be useful, but blended families in particular need to turn these experiences into memories that can be recorded and recalled. The sooner we begin to fill logbooks, photo albums, and treasure boxes, the sooner we'll feel a strong sense of history. We don't need to wait until something spectacular occurs. Remember the girl whose mother took her on a "lion hunt"? Or the family that dressed in formal gowns for dinner once a month? The more every-day moments we turn into special ones to be recorded, the stronger our new family identity will become.

It helps to pay particular attention to the QP factor "we could count on it." Traditions and rituals are effective ways to cement our new relationships. Many of the activities in Chapter 8 make excellent traditions and some take very little time.

The weekly family council meeting can also be a great aid in helping a blended family find its identity. Unless the child entering a blended family is an infant or in the early toddler stage, he or she will already have absorbed many rules and routines from prior family experiences. In stepfamilies, two adults with different ways of doing things are forming one family. The council meeting can provide a forum where everyone can discuss these differences and make decisions about how things will be done in this new family. Jamie Sakuro describes how her new family came up with a solution to a dinner problem:

> Dinner in our family was a big problem. Dad and us were used to just fixing a plate and taking it into the den. But after our families got together, we had to all sit down in the dining room and go through this big deal. We hated it. Finally, we got to talk about it at the family meeting and decided that we would only have to eat together on weekends and special occasions. On weeknights we get to eat in front of the TV like we used to.

Although the two families that have become the Sakuro family had very different ways of dealing with dinner, they avoided the common pitfall of criticizing each other's ways, for in reality neither was wrong or right, they were just different. The family then came up with a plan that was unique to them—the Sakuro way of eating dinner. The more issues they work out together in this cooperative way, the more they will build their sense of identity.

Dealing with Discipline

While discipline can be a difficult undertaking in any home, there are some special difficulties nontraditional families face. Many parents have never learned effective discipline strategies. Women, especially those who have grown up in homes where the father handled misbehavior, may never have thought that discipline was their job. Mothers or fathers, before their separation, may have let the spouse be the primary person to deal with discipline in the family and they may now be too short of time to remedy the situation by reading or by attending parenting classes.

Even those single parents who do possess good discipline strategies may not be using them. In a mistaken attempt to help their kids through a stressful time, and perhaps even to assuage their own guilt about the breakup of the original family, these parents think that ignoring some misbehavior will alleviate the pressure and make life more pleasant for the kids. In fact, ignoring misbehavior almost always makes matters worse, for it teaches children that they can do anything they want without having to face the consequences.

Children experiencing losses and changes in their lives often have adjustment difficulties that show up as very erratic and negative behavior. Some children of divorce go so far as to make a conscious decision to misbehave in an effort to force their original parents to reunite. "I'll be so bad Dad will have to come back home" is a ploy some of them use.

Children in blended families, also experiencing changes and adjustment difficulties, may behave just as inappropriately and the fact that there are now two adults in the home may not be an advantage. Many stepparents and foster parents are willing to take on the job of discipline, but this often backfires because the children refuse to accept the authority of the nonbiological parent. "You're not my *real* father," says ten-year-old Tammy. "You can't tell *me* what to do."

There's a direct relationship between these discipline difficulties and quality parenting. First of all, let's remember the bank account analogy from Chapter 1, where discipline is the side of the ledger we draw from. In other words, we first need the positive encounters to build up our savings account before we can draw from it and effectively discipline the kids. The role of the new stepparent, therefore, is not to be the primary disciplinarian, but rather to build a positive relationship with the stepchild, using the tools we have already discussed.

Unfortunately, this isn't simple. When kids are exhibiting a lot of negative behavior, we often become irritated and resentful. The last thing we want to do when we feel like this is to play a game or go on an outing or put our arm around a child. So a vicious cycle begins to form. The more the kids misbehave, the less quality parenting they get, which in turn leads to increased misbehavior.

The way out of the predicament is for us to separate the deed from the doer. If we can keep in mind that this isn't a bad kid we are now living with but rather one who is going through difficult adjustments, we'll feel a lot more optimistic about our relationship with the child. We can keep a more helpful perspective by making a list of all the child's positive behavior and traits, and otherwise looking for opportunities to "catch 'em being good."

We can't wait for children to change their ways before having positive experiences with them. We may have to take it slowly and pick our opportunities carefully, but it's not fair to think they have to "earn" the privilege of quality time together. As leaders in the family, it's up to us to step back, assess the situation, and make the first change. Once we've begun to break the cycle, we can expect that their behavior will begin to improve.

Chapter 11

QUESTIONS PARENTS ASK ABOUT QUALITY TIME

This chapter contains the questions that were raised by parents as we talked together about this book. They may also be helpful to you as you think about quality parenting in your family.

Q. *I feel so guilty because there's never enough time and energy for quality parenting. What can I do?*

A. Make some time each day, no matter how brief, to enjoy each child. Begin by concentrating on short activities, but at the same time, review your time-management skills. We really believe that all parents can find time for quality parenting. Evaluate how much time you're spending in quality activities on a weekly rather than on a daily basis. Some days you'll have less, some days more, but try to include a reasonable amount of quality time during the course of a week.

Most of us feel guilty when we aim for perfection and fall short. Strive for 10 percent more quality parenting next week than you had this week. Keep your goals reachable so that you'll wind up feeling satisfied rather than frustrated and guilty.

Remember, too, that quantity doesn't automatically translate into quality. Even if we spend more time at home, we are not automatically assured of more quality. Parents who work in the home have to make the same deliberate efforts to apply the ideas presented in this book as parents who work outside.

Q. *Can I spoil my kids with too much quality parenting?*

A. You can't spoil kids with positive interactions, as long as they occur at appropriate times. You can spoil them by failing to take steps to correct misbehavior, by overprotecting and pampering them, and by bailing them out of difficult situations they create for themselves.

It would also be inappropriate to use quality times to appease kids who nag, whine, and insist upon special attention in great quantities. By doing so, we would just be reinforcing this unpleasant behavior.

Some kids never seem to be satisfied. They are like bottomless cups—you can pour huge amounts of attention into them, but they never seem to be filled. If your child fits this image, set specific time limits for special activities in advance. When the time is up, end the activity—ignoring whines and pleas to continue.

Q. *Is there an upper limit on quality parenting, a point when there's just too much of it?*

A. Yes, there is. Kids need time to socialize with other kids, pursue personal interests and hobbies, complete homework assignments, or daydream. If too much of their out-of-school time is spent in activities within the family, these other important needs won't get met.

Parents also have competing needs. They must find time to pursue careers, to interact as a couple, and to fulfill personal desires. If they spend so much time with their kids that their other commitments and relationships suffer, they're not doing their kids or themselves a favor.

We'd have to say, however, that too much quality parenting is rare. In fact, we haven't met a family yet that has suffered from such a problem. The realities of the day-to-day time crunch keep this from happening.

Q. *Is it necessary to have quality parenting every day?*

A. It would be very unusual if, sometime during the day or evening, there wasn't the opportunity or desire for even one quality parenting experience.

Quality parenting can be compared to feeding our kids. They can survive a day without eating, but they will be physically hungry. Go on a quality parenting fast for a day and, though we and our kids will survive, they'll become psychologically hungry.

There are certainly times when circumstances will necessitate being apart from our children. When we're out of town or working very long hours, we may not see them for several days or longer. But even in such difficult situations, a little planning and creativity can turn up possibilities. A note of encouragement left under a pillow, a cassette tape with a personal message, a letter, or a phone call can act as a nutritious snack that tides a child over until the next full meal.

Q. *Should I concentrate on the quality parenting skills and activities that I feel most comfortable with? I'm afraid the others would feel phony and unnatural to me.*

A. We'd like to suggest that it's okay to feel phony once in a while. It's natural to be a little uncomfortable when learning new skills and techniques. However, the eventual benefit to our family and the great feeling of accomplishment that comes from mastering new skills are worth the discomfort. It's fine to begin with the activities and skills that seem most natural, but it's also important to stretch ourselves and try new things.

Q. *What if one of my kids gets upset and wants to quit during an activity?*

A. When someone gets upset, it's best to stop what we are doing and talk for a few minutes. We can use the sharing skills of listening and responding to identify the feelings involved. Once the feelings are out in the open, try to pinpoint the specific difficulty and see if a mutually agreeable solution can be found. If the child refuses to work with you, or if no immediate solution can be found, abandon the activity for the time being, without anger or resentment. Everyone is entitled to get upset occasionally, and activities don't always proceed as planned. Such an attitude will leave the door open to talk about what happened at a later date and to try the activity again later.

Q. *What should I do if my kids get carried away and an activity gets out of hand?*

A. This can easily happen. We're roughhousing with the kids and they ignore our requests to play more gently, until something finally gets broken. We're gathered together in a motel room and the noise level gets so high it disturbs the neighbors. Perhaps we're doing an arts-and-crafts project together and the kids keep dropping things around the house, even though they've been asked not to.

When such things happen, we recommend that the activity be stopped immediately. Clearly state what's bothering you and give the kids a choice: the activity can continue as long as their behavior remains appropriate (you must tell them specifically what is appropriate in the given situation) or the activity will end immediately. You'll see by their behavior during the next few minutes what choice they have made.

If they continue to be carried away, it's important to remain firm. "One more chance" is counterproductive—they just won't take you seriously if you don't carry through and keep your word. Kids will often continue to promise to "do better" but, as soon as we give in, go back to their inappropriate behavior. Ignore the promises and say there will be another chance, another day, to try again.

Q. *What if I suggest an activity that everyone wants to do except one person?*

A. If it's an activity that requires everyone to participate, like a family vacation, then the majority rules. But if, for example, a week-long beach vacation is being planned and Timmy would rather go camping in the woods instead, try to find a special activity, like snorkeling, that could make the beach more attractive to him. Maybe the family could camp near the beach, instead of staying at a motel, so that he gets to sleep in a tent. How about spending one afternoon taking a side trip up to a wooded area? Even the promise of a weekend camping trip the following month might help. Talking together and exploring possibilities will be more productive in the long run than ignoring Timmy's reluctant behavior.

Not every activity requires full family participation, If kids are adamant about not joining a particular activity, it's best not to make a big deal out of it, or to shame or humiliate the child. Perhaps the child needs time alone; the next time, he or she may decide to join.

Q. *Do I have to do exactly the same thing with each child and for equal amounts of time?*

A. While we want to be fair, it's best not to keep an exact score. We are only inviting conflict when we try to be even Steven every time. Our children will understand that if someone appears to have had more attention one time, it will probably balance out in the long run.

There are also times in everyone's life when unfavorable circumstances create the need for a little extra nurturing. It could be problems with a best friend, a disappointment in not being chosen for an athletic team or a part in the school play, or a poor grade on an important test. Whatever the reason, it's important to let our kids know that when anyone needs it, an extra dose of personal attention is available.

If any of our children complain when a sibling receives such special care, we can take him or her aside and briefly explain, reminding the child that such attention will be available when he or she needs it, too. Other kids shouldn't feel left out because one child's problems are absorbing all the family's time and energy. Sometimes parents can be consumed by special health or learning or emotional problems of one child. In those instances, a special effort has to be made for the others.

It's not necessary always to do the same activity with each child, because interests and preferences differ. One child may love to go shopping for three hours on a Saturday afternoon whereas another prefers a trip to the zoo. If each child is offered time alone with a parent on a rotating basis, the sense of fairness comes from the fact that each child gets to enjoy exclusive time with Mom or Dad.

Q. *My kids would rather watch TV than spend time with me. How can I entice them away from the tube?*

A. TV is a problem when it takes time away from more constructive activities like playing with other kids, developing imagination, or relating to other family members.

Certainly kids don't need more than one or two hours a day of television, and it's preferable for them to watch even less. Limiting TV-viewing and helping our children select what to watch is important. Make weekly viewing schedules so that everyone will know when the tube can be on and when it must be off. Being aware of these limits ahead of time will cut down on complaints later when the plug is pulled.

If we suggest activities just as the kids are settling down to a show or bargaining for an extra thirty minutes of television, it's natural for them to resist.

Q. *What if my spouse is not willing to plan or have quality experiences with our children?*

A. It's certainly preferable for both parents to join in, at least occasionally, but all is not lost if a spouse is reluctant. Remember, the emphasis is on *your* relationship with the children.

To encourage a resistant spouse to become more involved, it's important to avoid telling him or her what to do. Nothing gets less cooperation than nagging and cajoling. It's much more effective to let your spouse observe you enjoying special moments with the kids. He or she may feel left out and pick up on your example when it's obvious that something positive is being missed.

Another strategy is to invite your spouse to join a family activity that you've planned. The key word is "invite"—not badger or threaten. If he or she resists, back off and offer again at another time. Along these same lines, you can also build quality parenting activities around an interest of your spouse's. If he's a golfer, suggest miniature golf. If she's a music lover, find a weekend concert for the family. By creatively establishing connections between a spouse's leisure-time activities and family activities, you can open up the possibilities.

Q. *My divorced spouse is constantly having what seem like spectacular experiences with the kids, like taking them on trips or all-day outings that I don't have time or money for. How can I compete?*

A. Don't try. Most of the activities we have suggested cost very little and are not all-day events. In fact, most of the quality experiences parents described to us were not at all spectacular, but rather examples of good everyday moments. Often it's the simplest things that kids remember the longest.

There is a positive side to this question as well. Your ex-spouse may be overdoing it, but that's more desirable than having an ex-spouse who doesn't want to be involved with the kids at all. Eventually, he or she will probably learn that being a good parent can include some ordinary times (and even some boring times), and that quality parenting doesn't have to be extravagant.

Chapter 12

YOUR QUALITY PARENTING ACTION PLAN

> I've got a kitchen full of the best cookbooks you can buy. I've got a set of professional cutlery, and a set of copper pots and pans that spread the heat perfectly. And guess what I'm cooking for dinner? Hamburgers. Again!

As this parent knows, it's easier to learn the concepts than to put them into action. We have included this chapter to help you make that all-important leap from knowing to doing. The sooner we get started, the more likely we will be to implement quality parenting.

The four elements that enable us to make it happen are: QP factors, quality parenting skills, effective time management, and the activities themselves. How we blend these elements together will determine how much quality time our family will experience. The following pages will provide you with some tools to begin. Before using these guides, read them over, then involve your children in filling them in. The more cooperation you can enlist during the planning phase, the more cooperation you are likely to find in the doing phase.

Remember When

We used these cues in gathering information for this book. They can also help you uncover the quality parenting already in your own personal experience. Think about the following:

1. Your recollections of quality parenting experiences from your childhood

2. Your recollections of quality parenting experiences you have had with your children

3. Your children's recollection of quality parenting experiences they have had with you

In order to make use of these recollections, try the following steps:

1. Write down the recollection, including the activity itself and the thoughts and feelings associated with it.

2. Ask yourself or your children what made the recollection a quality parenting experience.

3. Then ask yourself what could you do to improve similar experiences by 10 percent in the future. Use the following lists of quality parenting elements to help make this determination:

Quality Parenting Factors

Parents spend time alone with each child.
The child is the center of attention.
The whole family does it together.
Kids can count on it.
Parents put kids' needs first.

Parents show they care.
Kids feel grown-up.
Everyone is relaxed.
Parents make it fun.

Quality Parenting Skills

Sharing
Encouraging
Playing
Teaching

Personal Profile

This profile has been designed to help you identify your quality parenting strengths as well as where you want to improve. First, rate yourself by checking the box that applies. Keep in mind that you can't improve all your skills at once, and that improvement, not perfection, is the goal. We recommend choosing one item to work on this week, one the next, and so forth until you are satisfied.

	Already Skilled	Need Some Work	Need a Lot of Work
Quality Parenting Skills			
Sharing			
Listening for feelings			
Responding to feelings			
Listening for the real meaning			
Responding to the real meaning			
Sharing yourself with your child			

	Already Skilled	Need Some Work	Need a Lot of Work
Encouraging			
Catch 'em being good			
Showing confidence			
Cheerleading			
Accepting your child			
Stimulating independence			
Showing respect			
Expressing love			
Playing			
Participating			
Making the time			
Being there			
Letting it out			
Tuning in to your child's delight			
Teaching			
Motivating			
Timing			
Demonstrating			
Practicing			
Acknowledging efforts			
Teaching the teacher			
Teaching values			
Time-Management Principles			
1. Make and use "to do" lists			
2. Alter the frequency of routine tasks			
3. Beware of diminishing returns			
4. Be willing to time-shift			

	Already Skilled	Need Some Work	Need a Lot of Work
5. K.I.S.S. (keep it short and simple)			
6. Chunk it, don't chuck it			
7. Make a written schedule			
8. Delegate responsibility			
Winning cooperation			
Distributing chores			

Activity Selection Guide

This guide lists each of the quality parenting activities found in Chapters 8 and 9. Use it to help select which activities you will put into action. After you check the ones you will do, transfer each activity to the Activity Planning Guides that follow.

	Activity	Check the Ones You Plan to Do
Morning	Reveille	
	Taped greetings	
	Reverse snuggles	
	Good Morning, America	
	Happygrams	
	Morning circle	
	Strong box	
	Fond farewells	
Before Dinner	TV critic	
	Sharing while preparing	

	Activity	Check the Ones You Plan to Do
	A family affair	
	P.M. Magazine	
	Accomplishment albums	
Dinner Time	Grace before meals	
	Table talk	
	Special honors	
Bedtime	Bedtime stories	
	Lullabies	
	Talk-and-touch time	
	Ending rituals	
Travel Time	Kids reading to parents	
	Tape time	
	Observation activities	
Special Times	Prime-time TV	
	Game time	
	Family council meetings	
	Dining out	
	Dining in	
	Holidays and family gatherings	
	Family outings	
	Vacations	
	Making memories	

Activity Planning Guide

The Activity Planning Guide on the next few pages can be used to help you plan and evaluate the quality parenting activities that you have selected. We recommend that you try one or two new activities each week, while continuing your previous favorites. Use the activities from the Activity Selection Guide and other resources, or create your own. The key is to plan, do, and evaluate.

Activity Planning Guide—Week of _____

Activity: _____
_____
_____

Evaluation: ___ Excellent ___ Good ___ Fair ___ Poor
What I liked: _____
_____
_____

What I didn't like: _____
_____
_____

How I can improve it: _____
_____

Activity: _____
_____
_____

Evaluation: ___ Excellent ___ Good ___ Fair ___ Poor
What I liked: _____
_____
_____

What I didn't like: _____
_____
_____

How I can improve it: _____
_____

Activity Planning Guide—Week of _____

Activity: _____

_____

_____

Evaluation: ___ Excellent ___ Good ___ Fair ___ Poor

What I liked: _____

_____

_____

What I didn't like: _____

_____

_____

How I can improve it: _____

_____

Activity: _____

_____

_____

Evaluation: ___ Excellent ___ Good ___ Fair ___ Poor

What I liked: _____

_____

_____

What I didn't like: _____

_____

_____

How I can improve it: _____

_____

Activity Planning Guide—Week of _____

Activity: _____

_____

_____

Evaluation: ___ Excellent ___ Good ___ Fair ___ Poor

What I liked: _____

_____

_____

What I didn't like: _____

_____

_____

How I can improve it: _____

Activity: _____

_____

_____

Evaluation: ___ Excellent ___ Good ___ Fair ___ Poor

What I liked: _____

_____

_____

What I didn't like: _____

_____

_____

How I can improve it: _____

_____

Activity Planning Guide—Week of _____

Activity: _____

_____

_____

Evaluation: ___ Excellent ___ Good ___ Fair ___ Poor

What I liked: _____

_____

_____

What I didn't like: _____

_____

_____

How I can improve it: _____

Activity: _____

_____

_____

Evaluation: ___ Excellent ___ Good ___ Fair ___ Poor

What I liked: _____

_____

_____

What I didn't like: _____

_____

_____

How I can improve it: _____

_____

Activity Planning Guide—Week of _____

Activity: _____

_____

_____

Evaluation: ____ Excellent ____ Good ____ Fair ____ Poor

What I liked: _____

_____

_____

What I didn't like: _____

_____

_____

How I can improve it: _____

Activity: _____

_____

_____

Evaluation: ____ Excellent ____ Good ____ Fair ____ Poor

What I liked: _____

_____

_____

What I didn't like: _____

_____

_____

How I can improve it: _____

_____

About the Authors

LINDA ALBERT is the author of *Coping with Kids* and *Coping with Kids and School* and is coauthor of *Strengthening Your Stepfamily.* Her "Changing Families" newspaper column is syndicated throughout the United States. She also writes a monthly parenting column for *Working Mother* and for *Family Magazine.* The mother of three grown children, Dr. Albert lives in Tampa, Florida.

MICHAEL POPKIN is president of Active Parenting, Inc., and originator of the Active Parenting video-based program, which has appeared on PBS. He is also the author of *Active Parenting: Teaching Cooperation, Courage and Responsibility*; and *"So... Why Aren't You Perfect Yet?"* He practices child and family therapy and lives in Atlanta, Georgia.